HAMLYN ALL COLOUR
GUIDE TO
HORSES

Designed by Town Group Consultancy Ltd

First published in Great Britain in 1993 by Hamlyn,
an imprint of Reed Consumer Books,
part of Reed International Books Limited,
Michelin House,
81 Fulham Road,
London SW3 6RB
and Auckland, Melbourne, Singapore and Toronto

ISBN 0 600 58013 X

A CIP catalogue record for this book is available
from the British Library.

Produced by Mandarin Offset

Printed in Hong Kong

HAMLYN ALL COLOUR
GUIDE TO
HORSES

HAMLYN ALL COLOUR
GUIDE TO HORSES

EDUCATION/HARDCOVER

HAMLYN

$\mathcal{C}$ontents

Introduction

To any dedicated horse lover there is nothing as fascinating as the wonderful variety of different types and breeds that co-exist in the equine world. That the mighty Shire and the tiny Shetland Pony should share the same characteristics that make up the essential ingredients of the genus *Equus* (the biological term for the horse) seems a marvellous feat of nature, with each breed adapted to the conditions in which it lives and the work demanded of it. How did this situation, which has been exploited to the full over many centuries by humankind, come about?

Sixty million years ago, a small, dog-sized creature, with four toes on its front feet and three on its hind feet, browsed the primeval forests and swamps. Scientists have given this animal the name 'Eohippus', after the period in which it lived. Twenty million years later, Eohippus had evolved into a bigger animal with three toes on each foot: there were two types, named 'Mesohippus' and 'Miohippus'. A gradual but overwhelming change in the climate, when the forests withdrew to leave open grass plains and barren steppes, brought about the next advance: to the first horse with single hooves, 'Pliohippus'. This early horse had eyes at the side of its head, for all-round vision to give early warning of predators, and teeth that could graze grasses instead of browsing on forest leaves. By one million years ago, *Equus caballus*, the first ancestor of the horse to bear true resemblance to the more primitive horses of today, had arrived, well ahead of the human race.

Equus caballus existed throughout America, Europe and Asia at a time when the continents were still joined by land bridges. Later, after the last ice age when the land bridges had disappeared, the horse became extinct in the Americas. But the rest of the world saw the emergence of three definable types of horse, each of which was to become the ancestor of a particular type of modern breed.

Two of these can still be seen today. *Equus Przewalskii Gmelini Antonius*, also called the Tarpan, evolved in eastern Europe and the Ukrainian steppes. It was a lightweight and hardy creature, of which the last remaining representatives are now kept in a herd at Popielno in Poland. This horse is probably the ancestor of most of the light breeds to be found throughout the world.

Equus Przewalskii Przewalskii Poliakov, the Asiatic Wild Horse, is the best known of the three. Once thought to be extinct, it was discovered in 1881 by Professor N. M. Przewalski and can now be seen in zoos.

Finally, the forerunner of today's heavy breeds was probably the Forest Horse, or *Equus silvaticus*, a heavy, slow-moving animal once found in northern Europe but now extinct.

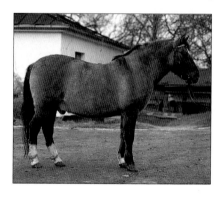

Equus Przewalskii Gmelini Antonius, *also called the Tarpan, is probably the ancestor of most of the light breeds in the world.*

The true history of the evolution of the modern horse is hazy, but further research has promoted the idea of four other subtypes that predated domestication by humans. These were Pony Type 1, resembling the Exmoor Pony; Pony Type 2, larger and heavier and possibly an ancestor of the Highland Pony; Horse Type 3, from Central Asia and similar to the Akhal-Teke; and Horse Type 4, a refined type from western Asia, likely to be a forerunner of the Arabian.

When the horse was first ridden by a human being is not known but that development was one of the most far-reaching and significant of all early human achievements. Suddenly, this puny, two-legged creature was imbued with power, strength and speed. Humans could travel long distances in a day in their hunt for food; they could spread their territory far and wide. The larger brain of the human, with its power of reason, and the horse's ability to move fast and transport people and goods, formed a partnership that was not only formidable but invincible in the primitive world.

Through the ages, the horse continued to be a mainstay in the progress of the human race, from primitive hunter to tool user and metal worker, from nomad to agricultural settler and, perhaps less nobly, to conquering warrior. The value of the horse was all-embracing. It provided not only transportation, but meat, milk and hides, with the minimum given in return. Being an efficient converter of food, a horse cost very little to keep and its diet was infinitely variable according to where it lived. In its different forms, it adapted to heat, cold, grassy plain, barren desert or rugged mountain. It also responded well to domestication as it already lived in the social environment of the herd. Had people designed the horse themselves, they could not have devised a more willing and versatile provider of all their needs, including companionship.

The psychology of the horse is a fascinating study in itself. Each horse grows up to know its place in the 'pecking order' of the herd. It is only necessary to watch a group of horses in the field at feeding time to discover which is in charge and which has to wait until last to be served. In a family group, the younger members must defer to their elders. Among those of the same age, trials of strength and 'play fighting' are common, to establish which horse will eventually be leader. Just as a young foal must respond instantly to its mother's peremptory call, so the schooled horse will be obedient to its master's aids when ridden.

Training is not just about obedience, however. The horse is as intelligent and responsive as its owner, handler or trainer allows it to be. By watching the horse's behaviour, listening to its language, which is often body language rather than vocal sounds (although vocal sounds play an important role) and understanding how the horse feels, the human can develop a partnership of rare quality and value with the horse. If you share your life with a horse that comes willingly when called, the ears of which prick up at the sound of your voice, that follows you without need

Equus Przewalskii Przewalskii Poliakov, *the Asiatic Wild Horse, is believed to be one of the ancestors of the modern horse. It can still be seen in many zoos.*

of a headcollar, that feels safe enough to remain lying down when you enter its stable, that rests its head on your shoulder, that, by its alert look, points out things of interest when you are out riding together, that will share your lunch, that will trust you and show no fear when you do things to it that are outside its natural experience and that will do things for you that it would not do in its undomesticated state – jumping, coping with traffic, putting up with innoculations from the vet – if you have a horse that will do all this, you have riches beyond gold and have understood the meaning of horsemanship.

All horses have characteristics in common, such as the fact that they are herbivores and therefore are not hunters but the hunted. Along with this goes the basic instinct of fleeing from danger rather than staying and fighting. Horses are social creatures, evolved for life in a herd, with its rules for survival which depend on obedience to the herd leaders. All animals, however, strive to pass on their genes through dominance over their fellows and the success of any individual depends upon how high up in the pecking order it can make a place for itself. For this reason, life in the herd consists of constant challenges and, until a relationship is established between a horse and its new human owner, there are likely to be challenges from the horse. All these aspects have developed to a greater or lesser extent in the horse breeds, which have themselves been progressively developed, both naturally and to a considerable degree by people, to fit different purposes and needs. It is no accident that there are so many breeds that this book cannot cover them all.

The English Thoroughbred is, perhaps, the supreme example of how humans have adapted horses for their own ends. It took 60 million years for the horse to evolve to the point where it became recognizable as the animal we know today, yet in no more than the blink of an eye in evolutionary terms (about 200 years) a horse was created that has been described as the ultimate racing machine. Beginning with some basically good, sound, but relatively undistinguished, mares, plus a number of oriental stallions, a pool of horses was developed for no other purpose than racing. The prime factor to be encouraged in this process was the development of the horse's ability and, therefore, its instinct, to flee from danger. Its body became lightweight and streamlined. Its bones grew longer and its joints became more angled and larger, to accommodate the attachment of powerful muscles. In this single-minded search for speed, no thought was given to other important considerations, such as a calm temperament or hard, sound feet. In fact, by pursuing the requirement for quick acceleration and sprinting ability, breeders automatically heightened the horse's tendency to run first and think afterwards – thus the Thoroughbred became an animal of such explosively quick reactions that it can only safely be handled by experienced horse breeders, and Thoroughbred stallions, with their strong instinct to dominate added to the equation, are particularly volatile.

The Andalusian's influence on other horse breeds is exceeded perhaps only by the Arab and the Thoroughbred.

INTRODUCTION

The Breton is the most common of the French draught horses. It is a descendant of the steppe horses found in Brittany that were ridden by the Celts.

In contrast, the Thoroughbred's progenitor, the Arabian horse, although agile and with good ground-covering paces, has a wider outlook on life. Selectively bred by the desert Bedouin, and living side by side with them, in their tents as often as out, the Arabian became highly responsive to human contact and is probably the most intelligent (as humans understand intelligence) of all the horse breeds. As it lived with its master, this horse had to be docile as well as fearless and spirited when carrying him on a tribal raid, so that it combines many attributes and, properly treated, is the most gentle of equines. It is sad that people's misunderstanding of the Arabian often causes it to appear to behave badly, when what is actually happening is that it has become confused and upset by the inconsistent and conflicting demands of its human handlers. Whereas a less intelligent horse breed would neither respond positively nor object to such treatment, the Arabian's intelligence actually acts against it in the hands of those with limited understanding of horses.

This book attempts to describe the origins and reasons for the development of some of the most interesting breeds. Choosing a breed of horse to buy is no easy matter – some people are drawn irresistibly to a particular breed, others instead opt for a 'type' of horse that is suitable for their use. The distinction between breeds and types is growing ever more indistinct, as few breeds are 'pure' in the sense that they are not influenced by blood from other breeds, and this will be seen clearly in the following pages. The term 'type' usually distinguishes the use to which a horse is put, although it may refer to a distinguishing characteristic such as colour.

The most modern group of breeds, the 'Warmbloods', are of a type that has metamorphosed and are now regarded as a group of 'breeds', even though they have been specifically developed, through selective breeding, for a particular purpose. The many Warmblood breed names, based on the areas where they were first bred, refer to horses that are of varying origins yet are remarkably homogenous in 'type'. The terms 'breed' and 'type', therefore, cannot be used in too strict a sense.

Studying the history and development of the horse is a fascinating business and becoming involved in breeding itself adds new aspects to the equation. It has been said that noone has yet bred the 'perfect horse' and no doubt the quest to do so will continue as long as people and horses co-exist. Meanwhile, we have the horse as it is today – noble, proud, swift, strong, gentle and created, according to Arab legend, not in prehistoric swamps but, much more aptly, from the wind.

As well as detailed descriptions of the world's most popular horse breeds, interspersed throughout the text of this book there are helpful, at-a-glance notes which describe any distinguishing features a particular breed or type might display. The reader's attention is also drawn to the special skills of certain breeds or special techniques to look out for in their show presentation.

Shetland Pony

*B*est known for being the smallest of the nine British native breeds of ponies, the Shetland has thrived in the harsh conditions of the Shetland Islands for over 2,000 years. The standard for the breed was largely fixed with the formation of the Londonderry Stud in Bressay, Shetland, around 1870 and the Stud Book Society was formed in 1890.

Shetland Ponies do best on open, rough grazing, but can also easily be kept in small fields. They need hay to supplement the grass in winter and clean, fresh water must always be available. In their natural environment, they find shelter from bad weather in the lee of hedges or stone walls and their woolly coats keep them dry.

Shetland Ponies are very strong for their size but, properly handled and trained, they can make children's ponies that provide tremendous fun. In recent years, one of their main claims to fame is competing in the hotly contested Shetland Pony Grand National at the Olympia Christmas Show in London. They are as popular with show ring spectators as with their enthusiastic breeders. They can be trained to harness and driven, in an appropriately small turnout, and have found jobs as diverse as racehorse companion and regimental mascot.

SHOW PRESENTATION

The Shetland Pony Grand National is taken very seriously. Ponies are properly trained and clipped and their riders are kitted out in full racing colours.

HEIGHT

Not to exceed 102 cm (40 ins) at three years nor 107 cm (42 ins) at four years and over.

COLOUR

Any except spotted.

HEAD

Small and refined; small neat ears; large eyes.

NECK

Strong and short. Plenty of silky, straight hair on mane and tail.

BODY

Well ribbed-up, short back, strong quarters and high set tail.

LIMBS

Plenty of bone for size; short cannons. Hard, round, open feet.

Dartmoor Pony

An excellent riding pony; a willing, kind and obedient temperament sums up the attractive Dartmoor. ▶

HEIGHT

Not exceeding 12.2 h.h.

COLOUR

Bay brown, black, grey and sometimes roan or chestnut; no piebalds or skewbalds allowed and excessive white discouraged.

HEAD

Small, well set on and 'blood-like', with very small, alert ears.

NECK

Strong but not too heavy. Stallions have a moderate crest.

SHOULDERS

Well-laid back, giving a good front.

BODY

Back, loins and hindquarters strong and well-covered with muscle.

FEET

Tough and well-shaped.

TAIL

Set high and full.

ACTION

Low, free, typical hack or riding action.

A 'miniature middleweight hunter' is a description often applied to this most attractive of the small native breeds, the Dartmoor Pony. Hailing from the wild and granite-strewn moorlands of south west England, the 'Dartie' is both hardy in its natural environment and eminently adaptable to domestic use. The earliest record of the breed is found in the will of a Saxon bishop, Aefwold of Crediton, dated 1012. In 1296-7, a fee of twopence was charged for pasturing ponies on the moor. Later, the ponies were traditionally used for carrying tin mined on the moor to the stannary towns for weighing. From 1902, registration was refused to any pony with more than a quarter alien blood, until, after the depredations on the breed by the First World War, the most influential sire of the modern-day Dartmoor, The Leat, sired by a desert-bred Arab, Dwarka, was accepted. He produced three very successful daughters, through whom most of today's ponies trace their lineage.

The numbers registered are not large, but breeding of purebreds has always tended to be very selective, keeping historic lines going and the bloodlines true to type.

The Dartmoor's equable nature makes it an ideal first pony and its relatively small size means that it is easy for a child to handle, yet it is athletic and forward-going enough to give an older child pleasure in Pony Club activities, hunting or jumping. Small Dartmoors have also been very successful when driven in harness and are a picture in the show ring.

Exmoor Pony

◄ *The efforts of the Rare Breeds Survival Trust and the Exmoor Pony Society have ensured a foreseeable future for the breed.*

Although the Exmoor Pony Society was not formed until 1921 and the first stud book was not produced until 1963, the Exmoor Pony is firmly established as the most ancient of the British natives. It is the only breed to possess jaw development similar to fossilized bones dating back 100,000 years. Prior to the formation of the breed society, the National Pony Society began registering purebred Exmoors in the late 1800s. So few purebred ponies remained after the Second World War that the Exmoor was designated a rare breed, by the Rare Breeds Survival Trust.

There are three main strains within the breed today, the best known of which is the Anchor Herd, descended from a herd originally established on Winsford Hill by Sir Richard Acland, the last warden of the Exmoor Royal Forest. The other strains are Herd 12, a pure strain though small in number, and Herd 23, typified by the stronger-built pony. All registered ponies are branded with a star on the shoulder and, below this, the herd number, with the pony's number on its near flank.

Exmoor ponies are extremely strong and, as they are capable of carrying light adults as well as children, make ideal family ponies for all kinds of equestrian pursuits, notably for hunting on their native Exmoor.

DISTINGUISHING FEATURES

The Exmoor Pony's head is unique in shape, having a prominent 'toad eye' and a light-coloured or 'mealy' muzzle.

HEIGHT

Mares not to exceed 12.2 h.h; stallions 12.3 h.h.

COLOUR

Bay, brown or dun, with mealy markings on muzzle, around eyes and inside flanks; no white markings permitted.

HEAD

Wide forehead; short thick ears, 'toad' eye.

LIMBS

Clean, short and strong.

New Forest Pony

◀ *The New Forest is an extremely versatile pony, capable of carrying both children and adults.*

HEIGHT

Maximum height 14.2 h.h.

COLOUR

Any except piebald, skewbald or blue-eyed cream. White markings permitted on head and legs.

HEAD

Pony type.

SHOULDERS

Long and sloping.

BODY

Good depth with strong quarters.

LIMBS

Straight with plenty of bone.

FEET

Hard and round.

The New Forest is a large, unenclosed area of Hampshire in southern England. It was once an ancient royal hunting ground and survives today as a modern wilderness and National Park in the midst of a highly populated, commercial and industrial region. The indigenous New Forest Pony plays its role in maintaining its historic habitat, although a delicate and critical balance of stocking and land use must be maintained to preserve and control the traditional forest environment.

The New Forest, perhaps more than any other breed, has been influenced by crossbreeding, mainly in the late 19th century. An improvement society was formed in 1891 and, in 1906, the Burley and District New Forest Pony and Cattle Breeding Society began to register mares and youngstock. The two local societies amalgamated in 1938 and are now known as the New Forest Pony and Cattle Breeding Society. Since the mid-1930s no outside blood has been permitted. The demand for New Forest Ponies has led to the formation of a significant number of breeding studs outside the New Forest itself, and today riding ponies are exported to many countries.

The New Forest may not be as immediately recognizable as other breeds since all colours except piebald, skewbald and blue-eyed cream are allowed, but their good temperament, speed and agility mark them out. Their uses include dressage, polo, distance riding, cross country and jumping. Forest-bred ponies have no fear of traffic, having become accustomed to it at an early age and they are therefore ideal for driving in harness.

Highland Pony

*T*he Highland Pony is one of the oldest British native breeds and is possibly descended from the primitive North European Horse. Its principal use is as a weight carrier, for which it is superbly adapted.

Over the centuries, the Highland has been influenced by the introduction of Clydesdale, French and Oriental blood, the latter introduced as early as the 1500s by the Dukes of Atholl, who established one of the earliest formal studs. In the 1800s, a Department of Agriculture stud of sires was established at Inverness, for use by crofters for their mares. Pedigree records have been kept here since 1896, although the Highland Pony Society itself was not formed until 1923.

The Highland has a firm connection with the British Royal Family, through a stud kept at Balmoral. Apart from strength, the Highland's most notable quality is its placid temperament, which makes it particularly suitable for use by the Riding for the Disabled Association, both as a mount for disabled riders and in pulling special carts designed to take wheelchairs. Its sturdy, attractive appearance also makes it a favourite for drawing wedding carriages and similar ceremonial uses as well as an ideal all-round family mount.

⬤ SPECIAL SKILLS

The Highland Pony still performs its traditional role as a pack animal, and is used to carry the deer stalker's kill down from the glen.

HEIGHT

13-14.2 h.h

COLOUR

Dun (mouse, yellow, grey, cream, fox), also grey, brown, black and occasionally bay or liver chestnut with silver mane and tail. Dorsal stripe and zebra markings on the forelegs are common. Small star permissible.

HEAD

Broad between alert, kindly eyes, nostrils wide.

NECK

Strong, not short, with a good arched topline.

SHOULDERS

Well-sloped with pronounced withers.

BODY

Compact with deep chest, well-sprung ribs and powerful quarters.

LIMBS

Flat, hard bone, stong forearms, broad knees, short cannons and well-shaped, dark hooves.

PONIES (BRITISH NATIVE)

Connemara Pony

The Connemara has adapted to many variations of environment and climate. ▶

The exposed western seaboard of Ireland, with its mountainous bogs and moorland north of Galway Bay, is the home of the Connemara Pony. It is an environment that has encouraged the characteristic qualities of hardiness, agility and intelligence attributable to this popular breed. Subsisting on the rough mountain herbage, the ponies were once indispensable in the struggle for survival of the local farming population, carrying out all the duties of the farm horse.

In the days of Spanish commercial trade with Ireland, it is thought that imported Spanish Barb and Andalusian horses exerted a beneficial influence on the breed, and as late as the mid-19th century Arab blood was being judiciously introduced. In 1891, further influence was exerted by the importation of Welsh stallions.

The Connemara Breeders Society was founded in 1923. Since then, many Connemara Ponies have been exported and breed societies have been formed in many countries, including England and America. Its jumping ability is renowned and, when used as a cross, the breed has produced some notable stars, such as the show jumper Dundrum, dressage horse Little Model and, more recently, the eventer The Done Thing. Despite its 'riding' conformation, the Connemara can equally well provide a keen and agile, yet calm, driving pony, up to FEI competition level.

HEIGHT

13-14 h.h.

COLOUR

Grey, black, bay, brown, dun, occasional roans and chestnuts.

HEAD AND NECK

Well-balanced.

BODY

Compact, deep and covering a lot of ground.

LIMBS

Short legs, with clean, hard, flat bone, measuring approximately 18-20 cm (7-8 in) below the knee.

SPECIAL SKILLS

Children's show jumping is a popular sport, and one at which the Connemara Pony excels.

Fell Pony

From the west side of the Pennines, the high, bleak moorland overlooking the beautiful Lake District, comes the Fell Pony. The extremes of climate have ensured that only the fittest animals survived, producing the strong, alert, vigorous ponies that were the foundation of the modern breed.

In Roman times the breed was strongly influenced by Friesian horses, which imbued the local breed with several prepotent qualities, including their black colour, equable temperament, a particularly good trot and a slight increase in size.

The ability of the pony to trot for long periods without tiring was fundamental to its use as a means of transport for farmers taking their produce to market, sometimes covering as much as 64 km (40 miles) a day. The ponies also had a fast walk and, with the advent of the Industrial Revolution, the demand for food in the growing cities saw droves of ponies, herded loose, carrying goods to their destination.

The Fell Pony Society developed from a committee set up in 1912 and today, the Fell Pony is essentially a riding pony.

DISTINGUISHING FEATURES

Excellent feet are characteristic of the Fell Pony. They should be round and well-shaped and made of hard, 'blue' horn, surmounted by plenty of fine, silky feather.

HEIGHT

Maximum 14 h.h.

COLOUR

Black, brown, bay and grey. A star or a little white on a hind heel is allowed but much white on the face or legs indicates cross-breeding.

HEAD

Small, with large nostrils, large, bright eyes and short ears.

SHOULDERS

Sloping.

BODY

Strong and deep, with well-muscled quarters.

LIMBS

Strong, with plenty of flat bone and fine, silky feather.

FEET

Round, with the characteristic blue horn.

ACTION

Long stride with good knee and hock action.

Dales Pony

The Dales Pony is ideal for both riding and driving. ▶

HEIGHT

Maximum 14.2 h.h

COLOUR

Predominantly black, with some brown, grey, bay and, rarely, roan.

HEAD

Neat, showing no dish but broad between the eyes; muzzle relatively small; incurving 'pony' ears.

NECK

Muscular, of ample length. Long foretop, mane (and tail) of straight hair.

SHOULDERS

Sloping.

BODY

Short-coupled with strong loins and lengthy, powerful quarters.

LIMBS

Dense, flat bone (average 20-23 cm or 8-9 in) with ample, silky, straight feather.

FEET

Hard, round, open and well-shaped.

ACTION

Straight and true, really using knees and hocks.

The Dales Pony, the slightly bigger, near relative of the Fell, was bred on the eastern side of the Pennines. The early influence of the Scottish Galloway brought qualities of speed over rough ground, strength and sure-footedness – ideal attributes in an animal the purpose of which was to serve as a pack pony for transporting lead from smelting works on the moorland to the north east coast.

Like the Fell Pony, when the mines disappeared, the Dales Pony readily turned to farmwork. When trotting races became popular in the late 18th century, Norfolk Roadster blood was introduced – most notably via the famous Shales line – which further improved the fast Dales trot. A demand for vanners and gunners in the early 1900s saw the introduction of some Clydesdale blood, which threatened the pure characteristics of the breed, and the Dales Improvement Society was set up in 1916, together with a stud book.

Although bred mainly as a working pony, the Dales also makes a strong, agile mount, with a kind temperament. Its stamina, determination and ground-covering ability make it a useful cross in producing endurance horses, and it is versatile enough for other equestrian sports. The Dales Pony excels in driving competitions.

SHOW PRESENTATION

Dales Ponies are shown with full, flowing manes and tails which often reach the ground. When grooming, great care is taken to avoid breaking the long hairs.

Welsh Mountain Pony

HEIGHT

Not exceeding 12 h.h.

COLOUR

Any, except piebald and skewbald.

HEAD

Small, clean-cut; eyes bold; ears small and pointed; nostrils prominent.

NECK

Long, well-carried and moderately lean in mares but inclined to be cresty in stallions.

SHOULDERS

Long and sloping.

BODY

Back and loins strong and well-coupled, with the girth deep; hindquarters long and fine.

LIMBS

Forelegs set square, with long, strong forearms, well-developed at the knee and short, flat bone below the knee. Large, flat, clean hocks. The feet must be well-shaped and round, the hooves dense.

TAIL

Well set-on and carried gaily.

ACTION

Quick, free and straight from the shoulder; hocks well-flexed, with straight, powerful leverage and well under the body.

Tiny, but tough, the Welsh Mountain Pony (Section A), exudes the supreme self-confidence and charm that has made it a favourite all over the world. The forerunner of all the Welsh breeds, it is believed to be a descendant of ponies from Celtic times, winning from this heritage its remarkable qualities of hardiness, constitutional soundness and intelligence which have enabled it to survive in its rugged environment, often inspite, rather than because, of human beings. The wild ponies were a nuisance to the hill shepherds and many were destroyed following an extraordinary edict from King Henry VIII, ordering the destruction of all stallions under 15 h.h. and mares under 13 h.h., on the grounds that they were of no use in war.

Only at the beginning of the 18th century did farmers begin to realize the potential value of their native equine stock and the Welsh Pony and Cob Society was formed in 1901. Nine stallions and 273 mares were entered in the first stud book, of which one grey stallion, Dyoll Starlight (foaled 1894), was to have tremendous influence on the breed.

Today, the Welsh Mountain Pony is considered the ideal child's pony. It performs equally well in light harness and is immensely popular in the show ring.

Welsh Pony

The Welsh Pony's beauty and versatility makes it popular throughout the world. ▶

Few people today would see the Welsh Pony (Section B) as the ideal hill shepherd's mount, yet for centuries that was the main function of this slightly larger version of the Welsh Mountain Pony. They had to be well-balanced to carry an adult, fast to herd sheep and wild ponies, and sure-footed and economical to keep.

The Section B was developed with riding qualities in mind, thus a more sloping shoulder, good wither and length of rein were required, but the breed was still expected to maintain substance and bone. This was perfectly possible, despite the introduction in the 1920s of a few part-bred stallions of oriental blood, in particular Craven Cyrus who was by an Arab, and Tanybwlch Berwyn who was by a Barb and whose descendants laid the foundation of the famous Coed Coch herd.

A tendency to breed ponies that were too light and losing type, in order to compete against the more Thoroughbred children's riding ponies, has, fortunately, been forestalled, although many Section Bs still hold their own in these showing classes. Today, the best ponies combine the original qualities of hardiness, substance and good limbs with the finely drawn, intelligent features of the oriental horse. They make superb children's riding ponies in all spheres, from showing to jumping and gymkhana games.

HEIGHT

Not exceeding 13.2 h.h.

DESCRIPTION

Similar to the Welsh Mountain Pony, but, more particularly, the Section B is described as a riding pony, with quality, riding action, adequate bone and substance, hardiness and sound constitution and with pony character.

SPECIAL SKILLS

Fast, agile Welsh Ponies are the most popular breed for children's gymkhana games.

Welsh Cob/Cob Type

◄ *The flamboyant action of the Welsh Cob is its most arresting characteristic.*

The Welsh Cob (Section D) and the Pony of Cob Type (Section C) evolved to answer the need for a dual purpose ride and drive animal that could take a loaded trap to market, oversee stock and hunt all day. The Section C was developed by using small Cob stallions on Welsh Mountain Pony mares. It is no larger than the Section B Welsh Pony, has all the attributes of the Cob, yet is more manageable for a child to ride. The Section C is probably the most versatile family pony in the world, capable of every activity, with an enthusiastic, willing disposition.

The Section D admits the influence of Oriental and trotting blood, in particular through the sires Trotting Comet (out of a trotting mare), Cymro Llwyd (by an Arab), Alonzo the Brave (of Hackney parentage) and True Briton (by a Yorkshire Coach Horse).

Today, the Welsh Cob is valued as a driving horse, both in the show ring and in combined driving trials. It has influenced the development of various breeds and, crossed with the Thoroughbred, makes a superb competition horse or, with the Arab, an excellent endurance horse.

DISTINGUISHING FEATURES

The Welsh Part Bred Horse Promotion Group has been formed to encourage the breeding and use of competition horses that are produced by crossing Welsh bloodlines with others, usually Thoroughbred.

HEIGHT

Section C: not exceeding 13.2 h.h.; Section D: over 13.2 h.h.

COLOUR

Any, except piebald or skewbald.

HEAD

Full of quality and pony character. Eyes bold, prominent and set widely apart. Ears neat and well set-on.

NECK

Long and well-carried. Moderately lean in the case of mares but inclined to be cresty in the case of mature stallions.

SHOULDERS

Strong but well-laid back.

BODY

Back and loins muscular, strong and well-coupled. Deep through the heart and well-ribbed up. Hindquarters long and strong. Tail well set-on.

LIMBS

Forelegs: set square and not tied in at the elbows. Long, strong forearms. Hooves dense. Hind legs: second thighs strong and muscular; hocks, large, flat and clean, with points prominent. Feet well-shaped. Hooves dense.

ACTION

Free, true and forcible.

American Shetland Pony

The American Shetland derives from its British counterpart, but is less hardy. ▶

HEIGHT

117 cm (46 in) maximum.

COLOUR

Any, either solid or mixed.

HEAD

Refined and long, graceful neck. Ears short, sharp and erect. Eyes prominent.

BODY

Short, strong back, short-coupled with a reasonably level croup. Deep and full through the heart, well-sprung ribs and deep, roomy middle.

LIMBS

When viewed from the rear, hind legs should be parallel down to the fetlocks. Normally, the hind feet and pasterns toe out a little.

ACTION

The pony should walk and trot with long straight, prompt, balanced, springy, regular strides. There is a marked Hackney action in the American type, encouraged by growing the feet long and by heavy shoeing.

The American Shetland Pony falls into two categories: the Classic American Shetland, which is the older type of American-bred Shetland (although more refined than the original British Shetland following years of selective breeding in America); and the American type, which was developed from crossing, principally with the Hackney, to produce a miniature, extravagantly moving harness horse, which can also be ridden in various show classes. Despite its popularity, it is less suitable for a child to care for and handle.

The Classic type, however, is enjoying a comeback and its calm, stable temperament and willing disposition are listed as important qualities. The pony should have substance without coarseness; and the maximum height of 117 cm (46 in) at the wither is higher than the British Shetland Pony, while any colour is permitted. The ponies are hardy enough, although less so than Scottish Shetlands.

The American Shetland Pony Club was formed as early as 1888 and today has over 9,000 members. There are show classes at nearly all the leading state fairs and most major horse shows, and there are many different classes, both 'halter' (in hand) and performance. The stud book has a separate registry for 'miniature' ponies of 86 cm (34 in) and under.

Pony of the Americas

The Pony of the Americas is a purpose-designed mount for young riders, being a very recently developed breed which began with the foaling of Black Hand I, a cross between an Appaloosa and a Shetland Pony, in 1954. Quarter Horse blood has since been added and the breed standard, which is extremely detailed, specifies conformation comprising the best points of the Quarter Horse and the Arabian, incorporating the main characteristics – white eye sclera, mottled skin with irregular spotting especially around the nostrils, and striped hooves – and coat colouring of the Appaloosa. The result is a most attractive pony, well-balanced, with elegant style and substance, ideal as a child's mount for a variety of activities.

The Pony of the Americas Club, which is as old as the breed, has expanded along with the breed's popularity, runs a full programme of events for young riders aged eighteen and under and has recently introduced a 'Futurity Classic' for registered ponies of four and under, for exhibitors of nineteen and over, with classes including Western Pleasure, English Pleasure and Trail. Adults also may compete in Halter and Pleasure Driving classes. Show classes are split into age groups, the ultimate achievement being attendance at the annual International Show. There are now over 37,000 registered Ponies of the Americas.

DISTINGUISHING FEATURES

Like the Appaloosa, the Pony of the Americas has a distinctive white eye sclera.

HEIGHT

11.2-14 h.h.

COLOUR

Appaloosa-type coat patterns and characteristics, including mottled skin, white eye sclera and striped hooves.

HEAD AND NECK

The neck should be slightly arched and clean cut, with a distinctly defined space between the jawbones. Head proportionate in size to the body, with clean cut features; eyes large, kind and prominent; medium ears, alert and well-carried.

SHOULDERS

Deep, sloping at 45 degrees, with prominent withers.

BODY

Round, full-ribbed, heavily muscled; back and loin short, wide and well-muscled, with a long underline. Croup long, level and muscular; deep quarters.

LIMBS

Legs set squarely under body, straight and true. Clean-cut hocks, broad knees, tapering gradually into flat cannons. Medium pasterns and clean fetlocks.

ACTION

Straight, true and smooth. Should stride easily and freely with no choppiness.

Sorraia/Garrano

The toughness of the Sorraia pony is plain to see. ▶

The Sorraia is one of two native breeds of ponies in the area of Portugal and western Spain, which bred half-wild for many centuries on the plains near the River Sorraia, a tributary of the Tagus. The Sorraia is closely reminiscent of the primitive wild horse, and is usually dun in colour with a characteristic dark dorsal stripe and zebra stripes on the legs. It is a tough, hardy animal, living on the minimum of vegetation and, since the breed became domesticated, it has been used for both farm work and cattle herding.

The other native breed of Portugal and western Spain is the Garrano, which is smaller than the Sorraia and has similar origins to the French Gearron and the Scottish Garron. The Garrano is extremely hardy and strong, with good bone and plenty of substance, enabling it to carry heavy weights for its size. The breed is used mainly in light agriculture and as a pack pony, and it is to be found picking its way nimbly over the steep paths of the beautiful Traz-os-Montes.

HEIGHT

Sorraia: 12.2-13 h.h.
Garrano: 10.0-12.0 h.h.

COLOUR

Sorraia: dun with a black dorsal stripe and striped zebra markings around the legs. Also palomino and grey.
Garrano: predominantly chestnut.

CONFORMATION

Sorraia: a large head, with high-set eyes and often a Roman profile. Straight shoulders, weak quarters and low-set tail; light-boned limbs.
Garrano: Strong build for its size, with good bone.

Landais/Merens/Pottok

*T*he increase in popularity of ponies for children in France has led to measures to improve the native breeds and also to the development of a French saddle pony, based on native and imported breeds and the Arabian. All the pony breeds are listed in a common stud book, including most of the smaller British natives which have often been imported. National, policy however, is to expand the native breeding programme.

The Landais is probably the best known of the French pony breeds, from the Landes region in the south west of France. Standing between 11.3 and 13.1 h.h., this is a fine-boned, elegant pony, with distinctly Arabian features, particularly in the head. Colours are black, bay and chestnut.

The black-coated Merens is a sturdier type, from the Ariège Pyrenees and standing up to 14.2 h.h.

The Pottok, which originated in the mountains west of the Basque country, is altogether a much more sturdy, primitive type, and it has been used as a pit pony and for meat. When crossed with lighter breeds, however, it also makes an excellent riding pony. The colours are dark, usually black, brown or bay and the height is up to 14.2 h.h.

HEIGHT

Landais: 11.3-13.1 h.h.
Merens: up to 14.2 h.h.
Pottok: up to 14.2 h.h.

COLOUR

Landais: black, bay and chestnut.
Merens: black.
Pottok: black, brown and bay.

CONFORMATION

Landais: fine-boned with Arabian features, particularly in the head.
Merens: sturdy build.
Pottok: sturdy, primitive-type build.

Arab

HEIGHT

No limit, generally between 14.2-15.2 h.h.

COLOUR

Grey, chestnut, bay, brown and black.

HEAD

Extremely refined, with clearly defined bone structure, dished profile desirable; eyes large and dark; nostrils large.

NECK

Arched and cleanly modelled, springing from top of chest.

SHOULDER

Well-laid back, long and clearly defined at the withers. Chest deep and reasonably wide.

BODY

Short back; body deep and quite wide. Line of the quarters nearly horizontal. Tail carriage is distinctively elevated.

LIMBS

Forearm long and strongly muscled, with large, flat knees and short cannon bones. Hocks large and clean.

COAT

Fine and silky; skin fine, velvety and dark (pink under white markings); mane and tail fine and silky. Legs and heels clean.

Almost certainly the oldest breed in the world, certainly the most prepotent, it would be easier to list which other breeds the Arab, or Arabian, has not influenced than those to which it has lent its unrivalled stamina, courage, soundness, intelligence and, in varying measures, graceful beauty. Chief among these is the Thoroughbred – and thus the modern competition horse. With its floating paces the Arabian is a delight to ride, and, for anyone who takes the trouble and time to get to know it, a joy to own; intelligent, gentle, quick to learn and eager to please.

The Bedouin prized their Arabian horses and bred them selectively. Family strains were traced through the mare line and horses were named descriptively after their dams or their owners. The development of the Arabian breed in Great Britain began principally with the import of desert-bred horses by Lady Anne Blunt and her husband Wilfred Scawen Blunt in the late 19th century and the formation of the famous Crabbet Stud. The breed is the mainstay of the growing sport of endurance riding and in recent years there has been a resurgence of interest in the sport of Arab horse racing.

DISTINGUISHING FEATURES

The Arabian horse has a characteristically short, strong back, often possessing only 17 pairs of ribs instead of 18, as in other breeds, with five lumbar vertebrae instead of the usual six and 16 tail vertebrae instead of the usual 18.

Anglo Arab

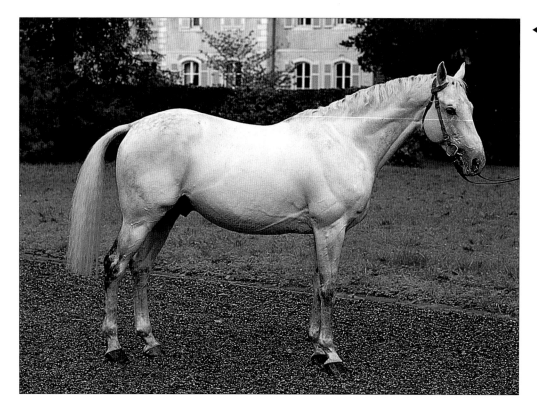

*I*f you want a horse that is a little bigger than the purebred Arab and with more athletic scope to tackle large obstacles, yet less volatile, hardier and easier to manage than a Thoroughbred, also one that bears all the hallmarks of quality, elegance and finesse, the Anglo Arab is the horse to choose. As the name implies, the breed was developed by crossing the Arabian with the English Thoroughbred, although this does not necessarily imply a straight 50/50 cross.

In Great Britain, Anglo Arabs range from pony size upwards and are of varied weight-carrying ability, so type may vary considerably according to usage. The minimum of 12.5 per cent Arab blood contributes to this variation. In France, the Anglo Arab is much more defined as a particular type and makes a valuable contribution to the pool of sport horses from which show jumpers, eventers and dressage horses are produced. From the early 20th century, breeding from established Anglo Arabian sires has added to the conformity and consistency of type. A further factor that influenced the French Anglo Arab was the introduction, in the mid 1800s, of a half-bred Anglo, a cross with indigenous French mares from the south west and Limousin regions, which produced numerous successful competition horses. The number of Anglo Arabs is small but many stallions are used in the breeding programmes of other breeds, for example, the Selle Français.

Apart from competition and pleasure-horse breeding, the Anglo has its place in racing in France, both on the flat and over hurdles, while in Great Britain, races for Anglos are a feature of Arab Horse Society race programmes.

HEIGHT

No fixed limit, up to 16.3 h.h. is possible.

COLOUR

Bay, chestnut and grey predominate.

HEAD

Profile straight; large nostrils and alert, intelligent eyes.

NECK AND SHOULDER

Strong, sloping shoulder, with more prominent withers and longer neck than the Arab. Mane (and tail) fine and silky.

BODY

Short back; deep chest. Croup often long and horizontal.

LIMBS

Fine structured but dense, good-quality bone.

ACTION

Supple and athletic in all gaits, with straight, true action.

HOT-BLOODED HORSES

English Thoroughbred

The prepotent English Thoroughbred is the result of a human obsession with speed. ▶

HEIGHT

Average around 16 h.h.

COLOUR

Bay, brown, chestnut, black and grey, the latter all reputed to stem from one line.

HEAD

Refined, intelligent with straight profile, large, alert eyes, large nostrils and clean throat.

NECK

Long, elegant and sloping.

SHOULDERS

Sloping and long, with freedom at the elbow.

BODY

Deep, with plenty of 'heart room', short back and powerful, muscular quarters.

LIMBS

Long, with dense, flat bone. Long and powerful 'second thigh' for galloping.

ACTION

Long, low, straight and free.

The English Thoroughbred was developed with speed as the sole criterion. Horse racing has taken place in Britain since medieval times and, according to the very earliest historical records, horses of oriental blood took part. The origins of the Thoroughbred therefore go far beyond the known pedigrees that trace from the three famous sires, the Darley Arabian, Godolphin Arabian and the Byerley Turk. From the time of Henry VIII, the situation was better documented and further oriental imports were used to improve the so-called 'running horses' that formed the basis of the royal studs and racehorses through the Elizabethan and Stuart periods.

From the Darley Arabian came Flying Childers and, four generations later, the great Eclipse. The Byerley Turk was the great-great-grandsire of Herod, foaled in 1757, the offspring of which won over £200,000, while the Godolphin Arabian was the grandsire of Matchem, founder of the third major breeding line.

Thoroughbred breeding today still concentrates on producing of a horse that will go faster than any that has been bred before. In equestrian sport the best event horses are now almost all part Thoroughbred and three-quarter- or seven-eighths-bred horses are the norm in dressage, show jumping, the hunting field and the show ring. The purity of the Thoroughbred's bloodlines makes it a suitable cross to 'improve' the quality of almost any riding breed. The National Light Horse Breeding Society encourages the use of Thoroughbred stallions to improve the national stock of horses bred in Great Britain by means of a premium scheme which makes good stallions available at low stud fees.

Shire

HEIGHT

16 h.h. upwards

COLOUR

Black, brown, bay, grey (roan – mares only).

HEAD AND NECK

Long, lean head, with long neck in proportion to body; eyes large, well-set and docile in expression; nose slightly roman; ears long, lean, sharp and sensitive.

SHOULDER

Deep and oblique, wide enough to support the harness collar.

BODY

Short, strong, muscular back, may be longer in mares. Wide chest, with muscular legs well under the body. Long and sweeping muscular hindquarters, well let down towards the thighs. Ribs round, deep and well-sprung, not flat.

LIMBS

Forelegs should be as straight as possible down to the pasterns. Hocks not too far back and in line with the hindquarters. Leg sinews clean cut and clear of short cannon bones. Feet deep, solid and wide, with thick, open walls. Not too much hair, fine, silky and straight.

The Shire is the plough horse of traditional rural England and the powerful beast that pulls the brewery dray. Decked in glittering harness, replete with burnished brass, with mane and tail beribboned in bright colours, it is a breathtaking sight and, although its origins as England's 'great horse' recall the clash of arms of medieval knights in their heavy armour, it is known the world over as the 'gentle giant' of the horse world. Certainly, it is only the Shire's docile nature that could make such a huge creature, weighing over 1 tonne, manageable as the willing workhorse of comparatively puny humans.

Influenced by Flemish blood, the Shire has characteristics that enable second and third crosses to make very good heavyweight hunters and even show jumpers. The traditional colour is black with white feather, and this was further established by the input of Friesian horse blood. The name 'Shire', from the counties of England where the horse was most often bred, is comparatively recent, the Shire Horse Society coming into being in 1884 to replace the English Cart Horse Society. In the 17th century, Oliver Cromwell called the breed English Black.

SHOW PRESENTATION

Horse brasses, used on the heavy horse's decorative show harness, were the traditional means of warding off 'the evil eye'. Original designs used traditional symbols of good fortune and protection.

Clydesdale

HEIGHT

Average 16.2 h.h.

COLOUR

Bay, brown or black, with much white on the face and legs, often running into the body. Chestnuts rarely seen.

HEAD

Open forehead, broad across the eyes. The front of the face must be flat, neither dished nor roman. Wide muzzle, large nostrils and a bright, clear, intelligent eye.

NECK AND SHOULDERS

Well-arched, long neck, springing out of an oblique shoulder with high withers.

BODY

Back short with well-sprung ribs.

LIMBS

Forelegs set well under the shoulders, hanging straight from shoulder to fetlock joint, with no openness at the knee, yet with no inclination to knock. Hind legs must be similar, with the points of the hocks turned inwards rather than outwards and the pasterns long.

FEET

Noted for their exceptional wearing qualities. Must be round and open with hoof heads wide and springy.

ACTION

Active movers for their size.

Clydesdale is the old name for the Scottish district of Lanarkshire where the breed originated in the 18th century, having been bred up from local horses, using Flemish stallions to give greater weight and substance. The aim was to produce haulage horses, following road improvement in the wake of the coal industry.

While there is evidence that the breed is a cousin to the heavier Shire, it is of a narrower build and lighter-bodied for its height, which has also given it more active movement without losing any of the hardwearing qualities of feet and limbs. In action, every shoe should be visible when watched from behind. Another distinguishing feature is the extent of white marking.

Like all the heavy breeds, the Clydesdale suffered a serious setback with the advent of mechanization, particularly following the Second World War. However, modern economic and environmental considerations now dictate a return to the use of the working horse, which, if well-managed, may prove more viable than a tractor or small lorry, so that heavy horses are currently enjoying a revival. The Clydesdale has also always enjoyed a strong export market and is valued as a cross for the production of heavy hunters and jumpers.

SHOW PRESENTATION

For showing classes, heavy horses traditionally have elaborate decorations plaited into their manes and tails.

Suffolk

Instantly recognizable, the Suffolk was the forerunner of the tractor in crop-growing country – and may still be cheaper to run.

The Suffolk has an endearingly rotund figure, carried on comparatively short, strong legs, which makes it the 'teddy bear' of the heavy horse world and certainly gave rise to its nickname: the Suffolk Punch. Its unvarying chesnut colour (traditionally spelt without the central 't') adds to the picture. It is most reminiscent of Britain's rural idyll, having developed specifically as a farm horse and is the oldest of the British heavy horses, existing unchanged since the 16th century or before. Its natural home is in the wide-open, arable expanses of East Anglia. Every registered horse can be traced back through the male line to one stallion, foaled in 1768 and called Crisp's Horse of Ufford. The original stud book carries an account of the breed, plus the full pedigrees of all the Suffolk horses alive at the time.

The Suffolk is extremely strong, owing to its compact and massive build – pulling matches were an interesting diversion from everyday 18th-century work and are enjoying a revival today. The clean legs of the breed make it ideal for working in heavy clay soils; it is also economical to feed, compared with other heavy horse breeds, has a long working life and is possessed of an excellent temperament.

DISTINGUISHING FEATURES

The Suffolk horse, with its 'clean' legs, was particularly suited to agricultural work, whereas the Shire and Clydesdale were more often used in towns.

HEIGHT

Mare 16.1-16.2 h.h; Stallion 17-17.1 h.h.

COLOUR

Chesnut: there are a few white hairs on the body and, in addition, a star, stripe or blaze are allowed. Up to seven shades of chesnut are recognized, these are: bright, red, golden, yellow, light, dark and dull dark.

HEAD

Large and broad, straight or roman in profile.

BODY

Deep all through, with heavily muscled shoulders and quarters.

LIMBS

Short with excellent bone. The legs are clean, short and strong, without any feathering like many other heavy horses.

ACTION

Active, straight and free.

COLD-BLOODED HORSES (DRAUGHT HORSES)

Percheron

The elegant Percheron is always grey or black. ▶

HEIGHT

Average 16-17 h.h.

COLOUR

Grey or black.

HEAD

Relatively fine, with square, wide forehead and long, thin ears. Lively eye, prominent sockets, straight, flat nose with wide nostrils.

NECK

Long neck with abundant mane and well-set withers.

BODY

Wide and deep chest; straight, short back and loins; long and rounded ribs; deep girth; full flanks; long hips and croup. Tail carried high in continuation with the line of the loins.

LIMBS

Sound and clean. Well-set and powerful forearm; wide and muscular thighs; low buttock; wide knees straight in line with the shoulder; wide and well-orientated hocks. Wide, flat, short cannon bones; strong fetlocks; clean and strong pasterns; not too wide a coronet; high feet, strong at the heel.

The Percheron is probably the best known of the French heavy horse breeds to be found outside France, for its versatility and many attractive qualities have brought it wide popularity.

The origins of the breed are obscure but the oriental influence is obvious and Spanish input is indicated. Arab blood has been introduced several times over the centuries and one rather touching description of the Percheron is: 'an Arab fattened by the climate and the hardiness of the work, which he has been made to do for centuries'. The principal input of Arabian blood was from the Royal Stud at Le Pin and the result of all these various influences is a variation in type that continues to the present day, with lighter and heavier representatives of the breed to be found.

Owing to this hot-blood input, the Percheron is a more graceful and elegant breed, with good bone, a sloping shoulder, more prominent withers and more active movement than many heavy horse breeds. This makes it an excellent cross with the Thoroughbred to produce heavyweight hunters and jumpers, and it has been used particularly for this purpose in Great Britain where the finer type of the breed has been further developed.

Its home, however, is in southern Normandy, a landscape comprising valleys of rich pasture with limestone subsoil and clay soils and a temperate climate – an ideal region ideal for breeding strong, healthy horses with good bone structure.

Ardennais

The Ardennais, from north-eastern France and Belgium, is an ancient breed which some believe to be a direct descendant of the 'Solutré' horse, which existed 50,000 years before Christ. In Roman times, it developed as a war horse and it continued to be used as an artillery horse during the French Revolution and in the First World War, as it was compact and more manageable than many of the heavy horse breeds, as well as being extremely powerful for its size.

Through the Middle Ages, its *métier* was as an agricultural animal and its breeding was influenced by the introduction of oriental blood. However, by the 19th century, agricultural demands for a bigger animal, of heavier bone structure and capable of working the heavy soil of eastern France, saw the introduction of Belgian draft horse blood and, at the turn of the century, there was a further input of Percheron, Thoroughbred and even Arabian blood, which saw the breed develop in differing directions. The main line was the short-legged, compact, muscular type, while, in the north, a taller, heavier breed developed.

Today, the Ardennais is found in most of north eastern France, from the Paris Basin to the Rhine and from the Jura and the Massif Central to the Belgian and German borders. It remains principally an agricultural draught horse with a niche in vineyard work and forestry, where its compact conformation and docile temperament make it more adaptable than bigger heavy horses. It is also used for meat.

HEIGHT

15.2-15.3 h.h.

COLOUR

Bay, roan, sometimes chestnut, dark grey or palomino.

HEAD

Large and expressive, with the profile straight or slightly dished. Prominent eyes and small ears which point forward.

NECK

Well set on and crested.

BODY

Shows bulk, density and power. Deep chest, strong back and loins with wide hips and long, muscular hind quarters with shortened tail.

LIMBS

Muscular forearm and legs with low, wide joints. Wide, sound feet.

Belgian Heavy Draught

The Belgian Heavy Draught horse, or Brabant, was an essential part of medieval life, but is no longer needed in modern, industrial Belgium.

HEIGHT

16.2-17 h.h.

COLOUR

Mostly red roan with black points and chestnut; but can be occasionally bay, dun or grey.

HEAD

Small and square; it is considered to be somewhat plain but with a kind expression.

NECK

Well-muscled, short and arched.

BODY

Immensely powerful and massive, with a strong, muscular, short back and great depth through the girth. Rounded, powerful quarters with a double-muscled croup.

LIMBS

Short, sound and extremely hard, with a great deal of feather. Feet are medium sized and well-formed.

The major importance of the Belgian Heavy Draught Horse is the contribution it has made to many other breeds. It originated in the Brabant region around Brussels, from which it takes its alternative name of the Brabant, and is a very old breed, closely related to the Ardennais. Both are descendants of the primitive, north-European *equus silvaticus*. Also known in medieval times as the Flanders Horse, the Brabant played a part in the development of the English Great Horse, the 'destrier' of the heavily armoured knight and therefore, eventually, in the Shire. The Brabant is a massive horse, yet at the same time remarkably utilitarian and sound for its size.

The breed also influenced the development of the Clydesdale and, to a greater extent, the Suffolk. In Europe, it contributed to the German Rhineland Horse and also provided a cross for several of the numerous heavy horse breeds of the former Soviet Union. It is little used now in Belgium, but has been a popular draught horse in the United States of America.

COLD-BLOODED HORSES (DRAUGHT HORSES)

Breton

◀ *The versatility of the Breton has ensured its continued usefulness, both in its native France and abroad.*

This is by far the most common of the French draught horses; a 1983 census numbered stallions of the Breton breed at 683 and mares at 15,381. Like most of the draught breeds in France today, the Breton is produced primarily for meat but in former times it was such a useful working animal that three types developed – the Small Breton, the Breton Draft and the Postier Breton. The basic breed derives from descendants of the steppe horses found in Brittany, that were ridden by the Celts. During the Crusades, these were bred to oriental stock and, by the end of the Middle Ages, two types had emerged, the Sommier from northern Brittany and the mountain-bred Roussin which was a finer type. Boulonnais, Percheron and Ardennais blood contributed to the modern Breton and towards the end of the 19th century, the introduction of Norfolk Roadster blood produced the more elegant Postier Breton. Since 1930, selection within the breed has been the rule.

Apart from its carcass value, the Breton is still used as a work horse on small farms, market gardens and for the more picturesque task of collecting seaweed, and its hardiness and power have made it popular not only throughout France but in many countries, including Japan, Italy and Spain where it is exported.

HEIGHT

15-16 h.h.

COLOUR

Usually chestnut or red roan, occasionally bay. It can be black, but this is very rarely the case.

HEAD

Square with a wide forehead, straight nose, open nostrils, lively eye and small ears. Sometimes dish-faced.

NECK

Extremely strong and slightly short and thick set, but well-set into the withers, with a long and very powerful shoulder.

BODY

Wide back, short and muscular; wide and double croup; rounded rib cage.

LIMBS

Very muscular forearms and thighs. Short and sound cannon bones.

Friesian

The Friesian typifies the universal appeal of the black carriage horse. ▶

HEIGHT

15 h.h. and upwards.

COLOUR

Black. No white markings.

HEAD

Finely shaped and very expressive, with small, pricked, alert ears.

NECK

Long, arched and well-proportioned with profuse mane (and tail).

BODY

Compact, strong and muscular, with sloping, low-set powerful quarters. Short and very strong back.

LIMBS

Strong, with short cannons and good bone, well-protected with abundant feather.

ACTION

Superbly balanced, energetic trot.

The Friesian, from the northern flatlands of the Netherlands, could be described as the world's original 'hairy' horse. Its glossy black coat, abundant, flowing mane and tail and profuse feather make it as attractive as any other 'coldblood' and its compact, sturdy conformation, with proudly arched neck, adds to the picture. Its origins are ancient – remains of its probable ancestors, which have been found in the Netherlands, date from 3,000 years ago. It was already well-established and its abilities proven in Roman times, when Friesian horses accompanied the legions to Britain and left their obvious mark on British native Dales and Fell ponies, which, to this day, are often black, with long, flowing manes and tails and have the same hard feet of blue horn. The 'Friesland', as it was called, also played a part in the development of the Shire.

Later, oriental and Andalusian blood improved the quality of the breed and it became a lighter, faster type, with a capacity for fast trotting, as demanded for the sport that became so popular in the 19th century. Unfortunately, this was nearly the downfall of the old Friesland and by the early 1900s there were few left capable of the agricultural work that was the breed's original purpose. The situation was saved by the introduction of Oldenburg blood and fortunately, the principal distinguishing characteristics were not lost.

Today, with horses seldom needed for agricultural work, the Friesian's prime role is as a harness horse. Enough have been imported to Britain to call for the formation of a British breed society and the breed is also well-established in North America.

Noriker

*I*n the Central Alps, where access for vehicles is limited, the Noriker still has a place as the working horse of the region. Sure-footed, sound, enduring and hardy, it performs all the necessary tasks of light draught and agricultural work.

Its origins can be traced from Roman times, when Noricum, from which it takes its name, corresponded to present-day Austria. The adjoining territory produced the Haflinger and although the Noriker is much bigger there is a striking resemblance between the two breeds; both have compact, powerful conformation and flowing manes and tails. A stud book was created at Salzburg around the mid-1500s and there is now a strictly controlled breed standard, combined with inspections and performance testing.

Like many breeds, the prime role for the early Noriker, promoted by the Romans, was as a warhorse. Later, an increase in size was brought about by using heavy Burgundian horses, but the modern breed owes its attractive appearance, refinement and excellent action to the ever-improving influence of Andalusian blood. Also from the latter came a spotted coat pattern, which is still sometimes found among the predominant browns, chestnuts and blacks.

HEIGHT

Between 16-17 h.h.

HEAD

Well-defined, intelligent, with wide nostrils and alert, high-set ears.

BODY

Short back, broad chest and great depth of girth; the girth measurement not less than 60 per cent of the height at the withers. Powerful hind quarters with well-muscled thigh and second thigh.

LIMBS

Straight and strong with ample bone and large, flat joints. Good, sound feet.

ACTION

Long and sure-footed.

Trakehner

Successful in all forms of equestrian sport, the Trakehner is powerful enough for show jumping, bold enough for cross-country, elegant enough for dressage and tough enough for endurance riding.

HEIGHT

15.2-17 h.h., normally about 16 h.h.

COLOUR

Chestnut, bay, dark brown, black or grey, according to the mare family from which it originates.

HEAD

Quality head, with wide-set eyes, neat muzzle; face often noticeably dished.

NECK

Elegant, long and graceful, well-set on good, sloping shoulders.

BODY

Powerful quarters, well-muscled with rounded croup.

LIMBS

Hard legs with short cannons and very sound feet.

ACTION

Straight and free at all paces, often extravagant in trot and with an athletic jumping ability.

The Trakehner derives from the Schweiken horse of the Middle Ages which later became the East Prussian, bred at King Friedrich Wilhelm II of Prussia's Trakehnen Stud from 1732. From the 1780s, quality, light horses were produced to fill the needs of the military. After the First World War, German military strength was limited by the Treaty of Versailles and suddenly there was a glut of unwanted horses. Gradually, this resolved into the use of the breed, still known as the East Prussian, as a dual-purpose farm horse. Breeding was carefully selective and performance-testing was already in force, so when the people of East Prussia were forced to flee the Russian advance in the later stages of the Second World War, they took basically sound, tough, healthy horses with them. The horses were harnessed to the wagons in which the people stowed what they could of their worldly goods as they struggled across the frozen countryside. From a stud book in which 27,000 horses were registered, only 1,600 arrived safely in the West. In 1947, an association now known as the Trakehner Verband was formed to save the breed from extinction.

The Trakehner is the only Warmblood breed the offspring of which are always called Trakehners, regardless of their birthplace. However, Trakehners are also frequently used to improve other breeds. The breed itself has been successful in all forms of equestrian sport.

Although the official Trakehner stud book of today does not include the old lines lost in the Prussian part of Germany at the end of the Second World War, many still exist there and have been used to improve breeds in Russia and Poland.

Hannoverian

For Warmbloods other than the Trakehner, Germany is divided into fourteen breeding districts, including those of the former East Germany, and the horses are named after the district in which they are bred, regardless of where their parents are from, provided they have been accepted into the stud book. Nevertheless, differences in the basic type are still to be found in the different regions and undoubtedly the best known and most successful to date is the Hannoverian. The official stud book dates from 1888 and the stud, established by George II of England at Celle, is owned by the state. However, the Society of Hannoverian Warmblood Breeders, which controls breeding policy in the area, is a privately run body.

The original Hannoverian was a farm and artillery horse, relatively heavily built. Later additions of Thoroughbred blood lightened the breed and produced an agricultural horse that could also be ridden and used as a carriage horse. Later still, after the Second World War, the prime demand was for competition horses and the introduction of further Thoroughbred blood produced the Hannoverian, which in recent years has become so popular in show jumping and dressage, and is exported all over the world.

DISTINGUISHING FEATURES

Warmblood horses are identified by distinctive brand marks, according to the area in which they are born. The Hannoverian is branded with an 'H'.

HEIGHT

16-16.2 h.h. preferred.

COLOUR

Any solid colour, white markings permitted.

HEAD

Increasingly refined as the breed takes on more quality.

BODY

Overall recent improvement, particularly in the shoulder and withers. Croup and quarters are becoming longer and more muscular.

LIMBS

Short cannons with good, flat bone. Hard, neat (but not upright) feet.

ACTION

Ground-covering but light and elastic. Improved free walk.

Holstein

Stallions competing with each other to demonstrate a breed's performance ability is characteristic of Warmblood breeding policy. ▶

HEIGHT

16-16.3 h.h. on average.

COLOUR

Almost always bay or grey without many markings, occasional chestnuts although this is not a popular colour.

CONFORMATION

Well-built, strong and muscular, with quality and depth. Clean, hard limbs with good feet.

ACTION

Powerful, with plenty of impulsion from behind and a somewhat elevated knee action. The better Holsteins produce elastic movement with superb extension.

The origins of the Holstein – heavy, native German mares put to Andalusian and oriental stallions in the 17th century – were the typical foundation of the modern Warmblood. Selective breeding, according to use, then accounted for the variation in type of the different regional breeds.

The small size of the Holstein area and its commensurately small numbers of stock led to the development of a particularly distinctive type of horse. From the original weight-carrying horse, a carriage type was developed during the 19th century, by introducing Yorkshire Coach Horse and Thoroughbred blood, the former providing the higher, rounded knee action required for driving and the latter refinement and quality. The Holstein today still retains a definite, individual stamp, possibly assisted by some inbreeding within a breed so small in numbers, and the temperament is willing but sometimes a little hot and therefore difficult to deal with.

As with other horse breeds, the later development of the Holstein answered the need for competition horses in all disciplines and Holstein breeders have been particularly industrious in publicizing their horses by competing them at international level in show jumping, dressage and horse trials. Stallions are included in competitions. For over a decade extending on either side of the 1950s, Holsteins ridden by Ritz Thiedemann enjoyed major successes in show jumping. A horse of particular note was Meteor, which won gold medals at two Olympics, a European Championship, a Hamburg Jumping Derby and a King George V Gold Cup in Britain, in addition to a great many other prizes.

Oldenburg/Westphalian

The Trakehner, Hannoverian and Holstein are undoubtedly the three most influential breeds in the development of Warmbloods in Germany and elsewhere. However, of the remaining German breeding areas, horses from the two north western regions are popular and have been widely imported to other Warmblood breeding nations. These are the Oldenburg and Westphalian breeds.

The Oldenburg was first developed as a coach horse, incorporating Friesian, Hannoverian, Norman, Cleveland Bay and Thoroughbred blood. As with the other breeds, this was gradually upgraded in quality and type to produce initially a lighter dual-purpose horse and later the competition horse of today, influenced mainly by carefully chosen Thoroughbred sires. Of these, Furioso, sire of Furioso II, established a line that is in demand in the United States. Furioso II, foaled in 1965, was a Selle Français and his was probably one of the most important influences on Warmblood breeding in the world.

In the early 19th century, a group of East Prussian mares formed a base for breeding Warmbloods in Westphalia and horses from this region followed the traditional dual-purpose agricultural/military use until military demand dwindled by the late 1800s and attemps to breed a heavier agricultural animal were made. These were not very successful and by 1920 the policy changed to concentrate on Hannoverian bloodlines. The Westphalian today is therefore, closely linked to the Hannoverian, with a Trakehner background, and provides an excellent competition horse for dressage and jumping, with some doing well even in eventing.

HEIGHT

Oldenburg: 16-16.3 h.h. average.
Westphalian: 15.3-16.3 h.h. average.

COLOUR

Oldenburg: generally dark.
Westphalian: any solid colour.

CONFORMATION

Oldenburg: heavier in type than other German Warmbloods, reflecting the coaching-horse origins. Powerfully built, with depth and strength, but now becoming a little lighter in response to demand. Limbs tend to be short, with short cannons and plenty of bone.
Westphalian: very close to the Hannoverian in type.

ACTION

Oldenburg: rather high knee action but regular paces.
Westphalian: powerful, correct movement and athletic.

Dutch Warmblood

The proximity of the Netherlands to Great Britain has provided the Dutch Warmblood with considerable influence on British Warmblood development and many have been imported for dressage and show jumping.

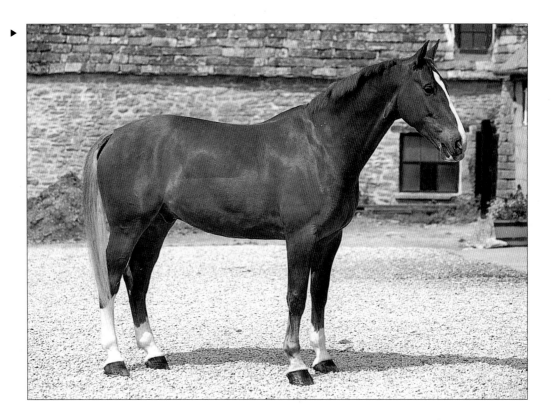

HEIGHT

16-17 h.h.

COLOUR

Any solid colour.

CONFORMATION

Reminiscent of the Gelderlander but given aristocratic quality by the Thoroughbred. Quality head, carried proudly on a long, well-muscled neck flowing into a good, sloping shoulder. Limbs sound, with good feet.

ACTION

Well-balanced and good in all paces.

Over the years, Warmblood breeding has prospered where there has been a recognized national or regional breeding policy for horses to serve particular needs and where consistent selection has been employed. This was the situation in the Netherlands, where agricultural demands had produced the Groningen, to work in the heavy clays of the north, and the Gelderlander, for the lighter soils in the rest of the country.

It was not until 1969 that the Warmblood stud book was established and it was also around that time that a large number of Thoroughbred and a small number of Trakehner stallions were imported to use on Gelderlander and Groningen mares for the development of the Dutch Warmblood. One of the Trakehners, Marco Polo, was the sire of Caroline Bradley's great show jumper Marius, who, in turn, sired the greatest jumper of recent times – Milton. In the next generation, Holstein and Selle Français blood was introduced. Although most Dutch horse breeding is privately financed, stallion selection through testing is rigorous and includes competition performance. The best mares are also performance-tested. How breeders then select their stock, however, is up to them.

Warmbloods are also increasingly being bred in Belgium, Sweden, Denmark, Switzerland, the United States, Australia and New Zealand. In France, the Selle Français and Anglo Arab (which is not entirely a mix of Thoroughbred and Arab) can loosely be thought of as Warmbloods, although it should be pointed out that the word 'Warmblood' is not interchangeable with the term 'competition horse'.

Andalusian

◀ *The Andalusian today is enjoying a well-deserved resurgence of popularity for the pleasure it provides as a riding horse.*

*S*panish experts believe that the Andalusian owes nothing to any influence outside of Spain, while some sources maintain that the Moors, during their long occupation of southern Spain, fixed and developed the breed by crossing their Barb breed with local horses. Whatever theory is correct, there is general agreement that this is one breed that contains no Arabian blood. Along with the Thoroughbred and Arabian, it has most influenced the world's other breeds.

When the *conquistadores* conquered the New World, they took Andalusians with them and their blood lives on in the Quarter Horse, Appaloosa, Saddlebred, Pinto, Mustang and possibly the Morgan in North America, and in the Peruvian Paso, the Criollo and the Paso Fino in South America. In Europe, the Andalusian was the principal forerunner of the Lipizzaner.

In the Renaissance, the Andalusian was the 'horse of kings' and features in many paintings of the time. Its strong build, coupled with proud bearing, elegance and unsurpassed riding conformation, made it the perfect saddle horse, an extremely comfortable ride in days when this was the only means of speedy transport. With a temperament of docility and gentleness these horses were a joy to handle.

HEIGHT

15-16.1 h.h. approximately.

COLOUR

Usually grey or bay with occasional blacks and roans.

HEAD

Majestic, with broad forehead, straight or convex profile and large, kind eyes.

NECK

Medium length, well set on. Mane (and tail) long and luxuriant.

SHOULDERS

Long and sloping with well-defined withers.

BODY

Short and strong with well-sprung ribs and a broad chest. Hindquarters are broad, strong and rounded with the tail set rather low.

LIMBS

Medium length, clean cut and elegant but strong with hard hooves.

ACTION

High and spectacular action. Possesses cat-like agility.

Lusitano

The Lusitano breed is sound, strong and highly athletic. ▶

HEIGHT

Generally 15.1-16.2 h.h.

COLOUR

Any true colour, including dun and chestnut.

HEAD

Long, noble with a straight or slightly convex profile narrowing to a long, finely curved nose. Large, generous eyes, inclined to be almond-shaped.

NECK

Long and powerful, deep at the base and set at a wide angle to the shoulder, giving an upright appearance.

SHOULDER

Powerful, with a high wither.

BODY

Deep rib cage, slightly flat at the sides. Short-coupled with broad, powerful loins and gently sloping croup; tail set low rather than high.

LIMBS

Hind leg positioned well underneath the body axis. Fine legs with dense bone.

ACTION

Excellent hock action and powerful forward impulsion.

The Lusitano is the saddle horse of the Portuguese part of the Iberian Peninsula and is probably as ancient a breed as the Spanish Andalusian. Afficionados claim that the two breeds are indistinguishable and that no distinction was made until the twentieth century, although some sources believe that Arabian blood may have been introduced into the Lusitano. Whatever the truth of the matter, the Lusitano is, in every respect, as useful an animal as its better-known relative. A war horse for centuries, used against the Carthaginian and Roman invaders of the Iberian Peninsula, it was also prized by the Romans and remained intrinsically a cavalry mount. In the 15th century, Lusitanos served as the foundation for the development of the Equestrian Academy of Naples.

While the Andalusian may tend towards a more refined appearance, the Lusitano retains the functional characteristics of a horse trained for combat, easy to manipulate, quick to turn and full of courage, qualities that stand it in good stead in its modern role of carrying Portuguese bull-fighters and working the cattle that are bred for the bullring.

Though it may be slightly less elegant than the Andalusian, the Lusitano's agility is unsurpassed and it excels as a high school horse. Naturally balanced, with its hocks underneath it, it is light in the hand and a joy to ride, with a temperament that easily lends itself to the discipline of a high level of training. Portuguese breeders have also found that crossing the Lusitano with the Thoroughbred produces a quality riding and competition horse.

Alter Real

The original Alter Real was developed as the horse of the Portuguese Royal Stud, established by the House of Braganza in 1748 at Vila de Portel and later moved to Alter do Chao, from which the breed takes its name. The Alter Real is based firmly on the Andalusian breed, the first horses to be bred being from a base of 300 mares imported from Jerez.

In the elegant period of the Renaissance, when the art of equitation as propounded by masters such as La Guerinière was at its height, the purpose of the breed was to be a performer of classical *haute école*. It was ideally suited to the task, with a spirited temperament and conformation derived from its Spanish inheritance. Many of the best horses were lost to the Napoleonic troops and the stud was abolished in 1834. The breed did not respond to the introduction of Arabian, Hannoverian or Norman blood as a means of reviving its fortunes and not until 1932, when the Portuguese Ministry of Economy took a hand and reintroduced the Andalusian influence, did the breed begin to recover and improve, to take its place once again as an *haute école* specialist, spirited and courageous, with a high, showy action.

HEIGHT

Approximately 15-15.2 h.h.

COLOUR

Usually bay, brown or grey.

BODY

Deep, with muscular quarters and of similar conformation to the Andalusian.

ACTION

High and showy, ideally suited to 'haute école'.

TEMPERAMENT

High spirited, less equable than the Andalusian.

Part-bred Arab

Often unacknowledged outside the show ring, the Part-bred Arab contributes greatly to all equestrian sporting spheres. ▶

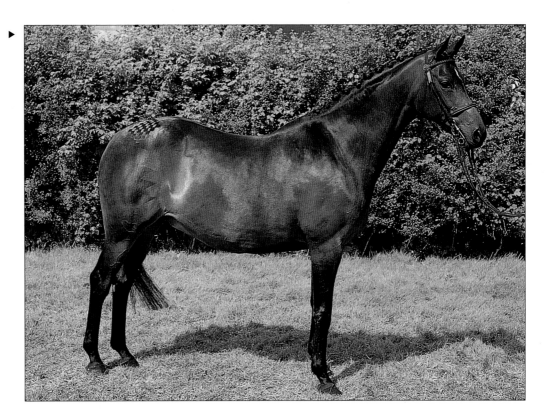

*D*espite being a tremendously versatile equine and playing an extensive role in all forms of equestrian sport and pleasure riding, the Arabian side of the Part-bred Arab's pedigree is frequently neglected or deliberately ignored because of prejudice.

The influence of the Arab on the better riding breeds of natives, from the small Dartmoor to the larger Connemara and Welsh Cob, is well-documented and it is with these three that it probably makes the best cross to produce competition horses and ponies for young riders interested in jumping and cross-country riding. Its gentleness and eagerness to please often make it a better choice of cross than the straight Thoroughbred for this purpose. A touch of Arabian blood adds sparkle and presence to the show horse and is frequently found in hack, riding horse and working hunter pony classes. In larger breeds, it lends soundness and courage to horses competing at high level in horse trials and it is the natural cross to produce endurance horses with a little extra size and power than the pure-bred, from other breeds, such as the Selle Français, Andalusian, Trotter or Standardbred, the Welsh Cob and Dales Pony.

HEIGHT

Ponies 14.2 h.h. and under; horses over 14.2 h.h.

COLOUR

Any.

CONFORMATION

Varies according to cross-breed, but characterized by wide, flat or slightly dished face; alert, incurving ears; large, expressive eyes; excellent dense, flat bone; often a slightly elevated tail carriage and good, hard feet.

ACTION

Straight and true with a springing step.

DISTINGUISHING FEATURES

The Hispano-Arabe has been developed in Spain by crossing pure-bred Andalusians with pure-bred Arabians, to produce a spectacular performance horse. Entry to the Spanish State Stud Book is strictly controlled.

Selle Français

The Selle Français is the pinnacle of success in the extensive French horse-breeding industry, which has been centrally organized and directed to make the best of the wide variety of breeds found in this strongly equestrian-oriented country. The main *raison d'être* of the breed was, and remains, its jumping ability and it is a strongly built, athletic but elegant horse. However, it is equally at home as a general-purpose riding horse or as a racehorse, taking part in the wide programme of races for horses '*autre que pur sang*' (other than Thoroughbred).

Not surprisingly, it derives partly from the Thoroughbred. From the 19th century Thoroughbred stallions were imported and crossed with French mares, in particular those of Normandy from whence the old name 'Anglo Norman' derived. Until 1958, when the official name 'Selle Français' came into being, all cross-bred horses were termed *demi-sang*, or half-breed. The new breed definition took up all the French saddle horse breeds, including Vendeen, Charolais, Corlais and Angevin. The modern Selle Français tends toward the larger end of the size scale and is defined in five separate weight classes.

Selection evolved into two main streams, the racing type, and the sport horse type and breeding is still carefully controlled, with the judicious use of Thoroughbred, Anglo Arab and Trotter stallions as part of the breeding scheme. The breed's most recent glory came when the little horse Jappeloup won the show jumping gold medal at the Seoul Olympics and, in terms of medals, this is almost certainly the most consistently successful breed in the world.

HEIGHT

Classified, as three-year-olds, according to weight-carrying capacity, as medium weight (small, 15.3 h.h. and under); medium (over 15.3 h.h. but not over 16.1 h.h); large, (over 16.1 h.h.); and heavy-weight (small, under 16 h.h.; large 16 h.h. and over).

COLOUR

Commonly chestnut, also bay, roan or grey.

HEAD

Sometimes a little heavy, though elegant and well-supported on a long, graceful neck.

BODY

Strong back with muscular loins and broad, powerful hindquarters.

LIMBS

Clean, strong joints, with excellent bone.

ACTION

Lively, supple and a good stride.

Salerno/Murgese/Maremmana

The powerful quarters of the Salerno denote its quality and ability to jump well. ▶

HEIGHT

Salerno: about 16 h.h.
Murgese: 15.2-16 h.h.
Maremmana: 15.2-16 h.h.

COLOUR

Salerno: any solid colour.
Murgese: often chestnut.
Maremmana: any colour permitted.

CONFORMATION

Salerno: generally good, with sloping shoulders, powerful quarters and correct limbs.
Murgese: well-balanced.
Maremanna: powerful quarters.

Although very much involved in horse racing, Italy is perhaps surprisingly not renowned for its native horses. The best of the Italian riding breeds is probably the Salerno, developed along Warmblood principles, although not officially recognized as such. It dates from the 18th century, when it was first bred at the State Stud of Persano which was established by Charles III of Naples in 1763. The famous Neapolitan horse of earlier times provided the foundation stock, together with the Andalusian blood, and the breed was subsequently influenced by Arab and Thoroughbred infusions.

Originally, the Salerno was widely used as a cavalry horse as it possessed the necessary combination of quality and soundness. Although rather unfortunately it is not immensely popular today, it is nevertheless a quality riding horse, with proven jumping ability.

Other Italian breeds include the Murgese, a breed developed in the 1920s, although an older breed of the same name is now extinct. It is named after the area where it is bred, which is inland from the Adriatic coast, and is primarily a light draught type which produces a good riding horse when crossed with the Thoroughbred.

The Maremmana, from Tuscany, is a much older horse than the other two Italian breeds detailed above, and is a tough, hardy, rather plain type, used for cattle herding and as a police horse, as well as for light haulage and farm work.

Barb

The Barb is an ancient oriental breed, distinct from the Arabian, although the modern Barb has been influenced by Arabian blood. Of North African origin, from Morocco, the Barb may have stemmed from an isolated group of horses that escaped the last ice age. Barb horses went to Spain with Muslim invaders as early as the 8th century and their introduction to Western Europe acted as a springboard from which the Barb has influenced many breeds.

The introduction of Arabian blood into the Barb breed has had little effect on its intrinsic characteristics – something that is unusual given the Arabian's ability to leave its unmistakable stamp on almost any cross. However, the Barb has certainly left its mark on the Andalusian, in the evolution of which it played a leading role. Barb blood was in the 'running mares' that formed the female base lines of the English Thoroughbred and, having reached Spain, it was taken onward to the Americas by the *conquistadores*. This exodus from Europe gave it an opportunity to influence the new breeds of the New World – the Criollo, Mustang and others.

As it retains many primitive characteristics, the Barb is not the most beautiful of horses, yet there is an appealing quality about its uncompromising appearance, emphasized by its inherent soundness and resilience, qualities that are all too rare in these days of refined overbreeding. It has a narrow head, often with a Roman nose, while the conformation of its quarters, with low-set tail and hind legs, would win no show-ring prizes, but it possesses depth, strength and courage – qualities that were prized in the cavalry horse and are no less useful today.

HEIGHT

14.0-15.2 h.h.

COLOUR

Bay, brown, black, chestnut and grey

HEAD

Long and narrow, often with slightly Roman nose. Mane (and tail) very profuse.

SHOULDERS

Flat and often tending to be upright, with rounded chest.

BODY

Deep, with short, strong back, sloping hindquarters with low-set tail.

LIMBS

May appear light of bone, but of proven strength and toughness.

ACTION

Quick, active movement, with stamina.

Camarguais

The Camarguais is now used as a mount for tourists visiting the Camargue, an area with unique wildlife and flora. ▶

HEIGHT

Usually about 14 h.h., seldom over 15 h.h.

COLOUR

Grey, usually almost white.

HEAD

Coarse and heavy for the size of the horse, with primitive characteristics.

NECK AND SHOULDERS

Short neck attached to an upright shoulder and flat withers.

BODY

Robust and deep; short back and strong quarters.

LIMBS

Strong and well-proportioned, with extremely hard, sound feet.

ACTION

Highly individual to the breed with a surprisingly long-striding walk with energetic, high action, a short, jarring trot, but an effortless, free gallop.

he marshlands of the Rhône delta in southern France, an area bounded by Montpellier in the west, Tarascon in the north and Fos in the east, comprise the general breeding ground for the ancient, small Camarguais horse. Its origins are unknown, lost in antiquity, although cave drawings from 15,000 years before Christ depict a similar horse, and skeletons found at Solutré in the 19th century are believed to be 50,000 years old. It is likely that the indigenous breed was influenced by the horses of various early invaders and later by Spanish and Barb blood from the Iberian peninsula. The Camarguais's hardiness led to its breeding being encouraged by the Romans and later it was recruited by Napoleon for his armies.

The Camarguais horse is tough and sure-footed. It is late maturing, but long-lived, with great stamina. When tamed for riding, its principal role is as a mount for the local *gardiens* or cowboys, whose work is to oversee the herds of black bulls bred locally for bullfighting (which in the Camargue does not entail the death of the bull). The horse must be nimble, quick-thinking and adaptable and the Camarguais is eminently suited for this purpose.

DISTINGUISHING FEATURES

The fascinating social behaviour of horses in the wild can best be studied by watching family groups, such as the Camarguais, which spend most of the time running free in their natural habitat.

Icelandic

◀ *There are about 73,000 horses in Iceland and the stud book is maintained by the Agricultural Society of Iceland.*

HEIGHT

13.2 h.h.

COLOUR

Various.

HEAD

Clean cut and expressive, with a straight profile and in proportion to the body; well-defined bone structure and veins. Ears rather small, pointed and well-set. Eyes large and set wide apart.

NECK

Comparatively long, supple neck, set high and narrowing towards the poll; full mane.

SHOULDERS

Long, angular and firmly muscled.

BODY

Wide, deep chest, well-rounded ribs and long, supple back with the loin continuing the curve to the dock and the croup sloping, wide and muscular. Tail carried freely, with hair long and full.

LIMBS

Muscle-bearing limbs as long as possible; lower limbs as short as possible. Joints strong, clean and well-defined. Hooves of tough, firm horn.

ACTION

Elegant, with light, effortless, springy and well-accented forward movement.

When the Vikings settled in Iceland in the 9th century, they brought their horses with them and from these earliest times rigorous selection was employed – not only by breeding policy but by the harsh climatic conditions of the country, which, between hunger and volcanic activity, ensured that only the fittest survived. For over 800 years, no further horse imports were permitted and the breed thus remained pure, retaining its ancient characteristics.

The horse was an essential part of life, being the only means of transportation for humans and goods. The Icelandic horse's excellent feet and the fact that, although small, it can easily carry an adult for long distances, bear testimony to its suitability for the task. Today, the Icelandic horse has a less taxing role – that of being a pleasure horse, not just for showing but as a means of exploring the rugged countryside.

The breed's long isolation may explain its predisposition to gaits now lost in most of the European breeds: 'the pace' and 'the running walk', or *tolt*. Not all Icelandic horses show the pace, with its lateral movement, but all should be able to perform the *tolt*, a four-beat gait that can accelerate to high speed while the back remains level, allowing the rider to sit without moving in the saddle.

DISTINGUISHING FEATURES

The four-beat tolt is a unique gait of the Icelandic horse.

Knabstrup

The Knabstrup is one example of a spotted breed of horse, deriving from Andalusian ancestry. ▶

HEIGHT

Approximately 15.2 h.h.

COLOUR

Spotted, with a wide range of colours and patterns.

HEAD

Kind, intelligent outlook with Appaloosa characteristics.

BODY

Straight topline, improved conformation for riding in modern breed, compared with the original strain. Mane and tail sparse.

LIMBS

Usually correct. Hooves marked by vertical stripes.

*S*potted horses have been prized in many countries throughout the world and various spotted "breeds" have emerged, although the coat colour derives invariably from Andalusian influence. The Knabstrup is one of these breeds. It was established from one Spanish mare, called Flaebehoppen, in 1808, who found her way to an estate in Denmark via a butcher named Flaebe for whom she was named, who in turn had purchased her from a Spanish officer.

She was bred to Danish Frederiksborg stallions (the Frederiksborg being the Danish quality cavalry horse, the original type of which has now largely disappeared), and produced a line of spotted horses of increased size, with brown or black spots of various sizes occurring all over the body, on a white background. The Knabstrups were intelligent, with a good temperament and were tough, though rather coarse and lacking in substance. Demand for them as circus animals led to concentration on breeding for colour, which almost destroyed the original type.

The redeveloped, modern Knabstrup looks more like the Appaloosa, with a wide range of coat colours and more quality and substance. It shares the common characteristics of spotted strains, such as the white eye sclera, mottled muzzle, striped hooves and rather sparse mane and tail.

Caspian

◀ *The discovery of the Caspian miniature horse in 1965 was an important landmark in the history of the horse.*

*I*t seems extraordinary that the Caspian horse should have been discovered as recently as 1965, at Amol in Iran, between Tehran and the Caspian Sea. Now considered the most ancient breed still in existence, it is thought that the Caspian may well have been the forerunner of the Arab, descended from Horse Type 4 (see the Introduction), which lived in western Asia. A horse similar to the Caspian is found depicted on artefacts dating from 1500 BC. The breed also shows several anatomical differences from other horses.

Although small and defined as a pony because of its size, the Caspian has all the characteristics of a miniature horse and is correspondingly very fast for its size, with the shoulder conformation of a horse giving it a long stride. Also, although rather delicate in appearance, with fine limbs and a narrow body, the Caspian possesses excellent dense bone, ensuring strength and soundness.

Added to this is an intelligent and willing temperament, making it a very good ride for a child, with the added bonus of an excellent jumping ability. It can also be used in harness.

HEIGHT
Between 10-12 h.h.

HEAD
Short and fine skinned, with very short ears.

NECK AND WITHER
Long, arched neck, flowing into high, sharp withers.

SHOULDERS
Sloping shoulders, shaped like those of an ordinary horse, giving a longer stride.

BODY
Narrow and slim, though with sufficient depth. Back straight with the tail carried high. Long, flowing mane and tail.

LIMBS
Fine, but sound and strong, with dense bone. Excellent, hard feet.

ACTION
Long striding, natural and floating, with great speed for the size of the horse and very athletic.

Quarter Horse

Certain strains of Quarter Horse possess what is known as 'cow sense' and are particularly suited to work with cattle.

HEIGHT

Usually 14.3-15.1 h.h. but can reach 16 h.h.

COLOUR

Any solid colour but usually chestnut.

HEAD

Short and broad, with small 'fox ears'. Wide, kind eyes; large, sensitive nostrils; short muzzle and firm mouth.

NECK AND SHOULDERS

The head joins the neck at a near 45-degree angle, with ample space between the jawbones and neck muscle. The neck is of medium length, slightly arched and blending into a sloping shoulder.

BODY

Deep, broad chest with wide-set forelegs. Short back, close-coupled with powerful loins, the barrel formed by deep, well-sprung ribs. Hindquarters broad, deep and heavily muscled.

LIMBS

Powerfully muscled forearms, smooth joints and very short cannons. Hocks wide, deep and straight.

ACTION

Collected, with hocks always well under it. Turns and stops with noticeable ease and balance.

Quarter Horse racing began in America in the 17th century, when the racetrack was the village street, the length of which was about a quarter of a mile. Thus the name 'Quarter Horse' originated. The breed itself, however, developed from Arab, Barb and Turk horses which came to the Americas with earlier conquerors.

The settlers' exodus to the west saw Quarter Horses turning to another type of work, for which they were also eminently suited. The long cattle droves required herding horses that could outmanoeuvre stubborn, intractable cattle and the Quarter Horse proved the perfect mount for the task, being strong and fast on its feet. In 1940, the American Quarter Horse Association was established in Fort Worth, Texas.

Today, the breed numbers over 2.5 million, making it probably the most popular of all pleasure horses. It is used in all the classic Western equitation classes – halter, Western pleasure, trail, reining – as well as in barrel-racing and pole-bending and the traditional rodeo events of cutting, working cow-horse and calf-roping. There has also been a tremendous resurgence of interest in Quarter Horse racing.

SPECIAL SKILLS

The American Quarter Horse can exceed 80 kmph (50 mph) during the classic quarter-mile race. 'America's fastest athlete' competes for over $50 million annually at 115 recognized racetracks.

Appaloosa

◄ *A quality Appaloosa with good coat markings is a highly valued horse.*

The spotted colour that defines the Appaloosa horse has been found in equines from ancient times. It was depicted in cave drawings dating from 28,000 years before Christ and through the ages such horses have appeared in equestrian art, carrying noblemen and other dignitaries. There were spotted horses among those that founded the Lipizzaner breed and Charles II of England possessed a red-rumped grey. Emperor Wu Ti of China waged a 25-year campaign against Persia in an attempt to seize the Persians' prized, spotted war horses. However, the origin of the breed is in America, where it was developed by the Nez Perce Indians and took its name from the Palouse River which flowed through the area in which it was bred. The tragic trek of Chief Joseph and his people, in an attempt to escape the US Army in 1877, ended after a 2,900-km (1,800-mile) journey during which Appaloosas carried the entire belongings of the Indian village. The Indians were defeated and the horses they had bred so carefully were slaughtered to prevent any rebellion.

However, a few descendants survived and the Appaloosa Horse Club was formed in 1938. Numbers have since increased dramatically and the register is now one of the largest in the world. Appaloosas vary considerably in type, from finer to more thick-set. However, they are versatile, with a kind and willing temperament, and take part in every kind of equestrian event, ranging from Western riding to dressage, jumping to driving.

HEIGHT

14.2 h.h. and over

COLOUR

A distinguishing factor, with five basic patterns:
1. Blanket: dark forehand with white over loin and hips and spots of any colour.
2. Leopard: white background with spots of any colour.
3. Marble: all over mottling.
4. Snowflake: base colour dark, with white spots over the body.
5. Frost: dark base colour with either frost or white spots on loin and hips.

HEAD

Straight and lean, ears pointed and medium sized. Lips, muzzle, nostrils and around the eyes generally showing parti-coloured skin. Eyes dark, surrounded by white sclera. Mane (and tail) often sparse.

CONFORMATION

Varies according to type, but should be compact, with good riding-type shoulder, sound limbs and feet, the latter often with striped horn. In America often similar to Quarter Horse.

ACTION

Smooth and easy.

Criollo

Polo ponies bred up from the Criollo are exported and prized all over the world. ▶

HEIGHT

13.2-15 h.h.

COLOUR

Usually dun with a black dorsal stripe but also blue or red roan, mealy bay, brown, black, palomino, piebald and skewbald.

HEAD

Broad but short.

NECK

Well-developed, broad and very powerful.

BODY

Compact, with a short back and powerful quarters.

CONFORMATION

Compact and muscular, with a short, deep body. It has plenty of bone, very strong joints, good legs and excellent, hard feet; very rarely unsound.

Throughout the world, the best horses come from ancient, prepotent breeds, adapted for the survival of the fittest in rigorous conditions, whether mountain or desert. The effect of climatic extremes in a tough environment, where the best must be made of the food supply that is available, is to weed out the weak and favour the strong. This situation certainly applies to the Argentinian Criollo, which, like many American breeds, developed from Andalusian horses imported during the 16th century. In the conflicts that ensued between European invaders and local tribes, many horses escaped to find their own living on the pampas.

Their descendants were rounded up by later settlers and named 'Criollos' a derivative of the word 'creole', meaning native but not indigenous. The Criollo became an all-round horse, the prairie and mountain transport and pack pony, and its soundness, stamina and ability to survive on very little food became legendary. Two Criollos were used by Tschiffely on his famous 21,484-km (13,350-mile) ride in 1925, from Buenos Aires to New York. The breed matures late, but is long-lived and very resistant to disease. It is the foundation upon which the prized Argentinian polo pony, crossed with the Thoroughbred, is based, and it can be considered Argentina's national breed.

Australian Stock Horse

The Australian Stock Horse is the modern descendant of the Waler, named after New South Wales, where it originated as the tough, versatile saddle horse of the Australian stockman. Perhaps it was typical of the essentially practical Australian pioneer that this eminently useful horse, that had played an essential role in opening up the outback, was never credited with any formal status in the shape of a stud book or breeders' association. The Waler derived from several breeds, most notably the Thoroughbred and the Arab, with infusions of heavy horse and probably some pony blood, and the result was an incredibly tough, sensible horse, comfortable to ride, agile and with weight-carrying ability.

While still busy in their original role, the Walers became much in demand as army remounts and in the 1880s many were sent to India where they became polo ponies and officers' chargers as well as artillery horses. This demand continued apace until after the First World War, when, in common with the rest of the world, mechanization caught up with Australia. It was not until 1970, when an invasion of Quarter Horses from America threatened to oust the Waler's traditional place as the stockman's favoured mount, that a group of enthusiasts formed the Australian Stock Horse Society. Today, the Thoroughbred is the strongest influence in the breed and, while still widely used on the huge cattle and sheep stations, the Australian Stock Horse is much in demand as a top-level competition horse, particularly for eventing and show jumping.

HEIGHT

14.2-16 h.h.

COLOUR

Any solid colour, with bay predominating.

CONFORMATION

Incorporates the best features of the Anglo Arab, with the head inclining towards the Thoroughbred. Well made, often with a suggestion of Quarter Horse influence and a stronger, stockier appearance than the Anglo. Exceptionally sound, tough legs and feet.

Akhal-Teké

Love it or hate it, the Akhal-Teké is a most unusual horse. ▶

HEIGHT

15-15.2 h.h.

COLOUR

Golden dun plus chestnut, bay, black, grey.

HEAD

Fine with large eyes, beautifully shaped ears and wide nostrils. Mane (and tail) fine and quite sparse.

NECK

Long, thin and set very high.

BODY

Long, lean and shallow, narrow hindquarters and long, muscular thighs. Fine, sparse tail, usually low-set.

LIMBS

Longish, slender legs, often cow-hocked, with small, hard feet.

Described as the national wealth of the Turkmen people, the Akhal-Teké horse is prized in the West for its extraordinarily beautiful coat colour of dun with a golden (occasionally silver) metallic sheen, which, in sunlight, is truly stunning. Chestnut, black, bay, brown and grey are also found.

This most unusual of horses throws up a dichotomy of conflicting values. On the one hand, it is a most ancient breed that has been kept pure over the centuries through a programme of careful breeding. The Akhal Teké resembles the evolutionary Horse Type 3 which existed in Asia before horses were domesticated. It can cope with extremes of temperature, as might be expected in a desert-bred creature and it has an inheritance as a highly valuable racehorse, as horse racing is a passion of the Turkmen people.

On the other hand, the Akhal-Teké is an example of a horse you would never want to buy on account of its extremely poor conformation. It is long in the back and loins, with a shallow body and narrow hindquarters. The legs are long and straight and the shoulder well-sloped, but the neck is set high and vertical, with the head joining it at an uplifted angle. The forelegs tend to be set too far forward, rather than under the shoulder, and the hocks are set high, so the horse looks as though it is standing over a lot of ground. For all that, the Akhal-Teké is lean and athletic, with sinewy muscles and an attractive, bold eye. Its powers of endurance are legendary – the stallion Absent won two Olympic medals in dressage – and it is also used in show jumping.

Tersky

The modern Tersky horse is a typical example of the thoroughness of Soviet breeding policy, which in this case set out to recreate an almost lost breed, that of the Strelets Arab. This in itself was a created breed, developed by crossing Arab stallions with Orlov and other mares, including some Thoroughbred influence. The vicissitudes of war and the revolutionary years almost wiped out the Strelets and the few that remained were taken to Tersk to form the foundation of a revived breed. Judicious crossing with pure- and part-bred Arabian lines produced a horse as near to the original as possible and the Tersky horse today is a proud, upstanding, athletic animal, larger than the Arab and of more substance, but with all the grace of the Arabian's spectacular movement and its proud outlook.

There are two types: a lighter-weight horse, more suited to racing and endurance, and a heavier built horse that is used primarily as a cross to obtain show jumpers. The Tersky breeds very true to type and the predominant colour is grey. The prepotency is such that the Tersky can be successfully crossed with many other breeds for various purposes – for example, Arabians, Thoroughbreds, Trakehners and Akhal–Tekés are most often used for the production of sport horses. Tersky stallions are also used to upgrade the native horses of Azerbaijan and Tadjikistan.

Although originally created at the Tersk Stud, breeding is now centred solely on the Stavropol Stud in the northern Caucasus and on some smaller stud farms in the same area. As with most other breeds, the Tersky is very frequently performance-tested on the racetrack, notably at Pyatigorsk.

HEIGHT

14.3-15.2 h.h.

COLOUR

Predominantly grey.

CONFORMATION

An eye-catching, well-proportioned, beautiful horse, very much resembling the Arab but usually with more size, depth and substance. It has elegant, floating paces, great endurance and an excellent temperament, making it popular in the circus ring and as a dressage horse.

Kabardin

HEIGHT

15-15.2 h.h.

COLOUR

Bay, black-brown, occasionally black.

HEAD

Long head, often with a Roman nose; sharp, alert ears and narrow poll. Thick, abundant mane (and tail).

NECK AND SHOULDERS

Medium-length, well-muscled neck, running into a flat wither and straight shoulder.

BODY

Short, straight back, strong loins, quarters sloping away from the croup.

LIMBS

Forelegs strong and clean with good joints and short, strong cannons; ample bone. Hard, strong feet.

ACTION

Comparatively high, with good paces; sure-footed and agile.

The Kabardin is a horse of the mountains, tough, hardy, adaptable and sure-footed. It is found in the northern Caucasus, the Kabardin-Balkarian Republic and the mountainous areas of Stavropol Territory and is a development of indigenous local breeds with Karabakh, Turkmen and Persian infusions.

Kabardin horses are kept in vast herds on the steppes, moving from lower ground in winter to higher ground in summer, when the herdsmen, dressed in their traditional astrakhan hats and *bourkas* (an enveloping cloak made of thick felt), live out with their charges, gradually moving them from one grazing area to another. In the spring, the herds are split into smaller breeding groups and, despite the numbers of horses, breeding is strictly selective. At foaling time, the herdsman must be particularly watchful, protecting newborn foals from the prowling wolves that live in these mountains. The people of the Kabardin-Balkarian Republic are fiercely proud horsemen, enthusiastic rather than polished! The idea that women should be allowed to ride is a novelty in this region and the riding horses themselves are always stallions or geldings, mares being kept solely for breeding. The herdsmen use a specially shaped, padded saddle, comfortable for long days of riding.

Although not a fast horse, the Kabardin takes its turn on the racetrack but is much more important in its traditional role, as a tourist mount or as an endurance horse in the competitions that have recently become very popular in the area – there is even an endurance riding association. The pool of purebreds numbers over 8,000 and the principal breeding centres are the Malokarachaevski and Malkinski Studs.

Budyonny

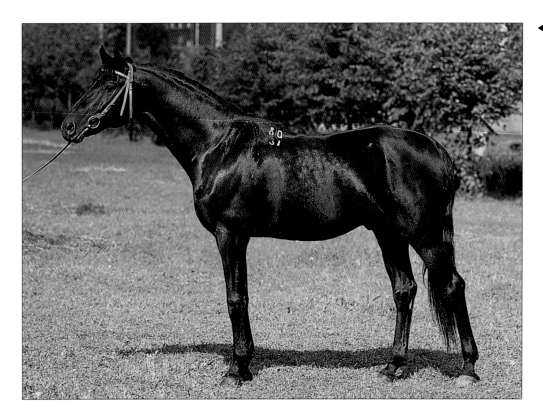

◄ *The powerful Budyonny is a typical Russian sporting horse and has an attractive, calm temperament.*

*D*eveloped as a cavalry remount, the Budyonny horse is now one of Russia's most popularly exported equine breeds, capable as it is of fulfilling many roles – as a show jumper, event or dressage horse, or as a strong and willing hunter.

The breed was developed in the 1920s and officially established in 1949, the breeding centres then being the Budyonny and First Mounted Army Studs in the Rostov region. The foundation stock was based on Don and Chernomor (similar to the Don) mares, with a large injection of Thoroughbred blood. The best of care was administered and the progeny of the breeding policy tested in the usual Russian fashion on the racetrack. The result is a versatile horse of Thoroughbred type, although comparatively light of bone and heavy of body. Perhaps surprisingly, the breed has proved to have exceptional stamina, with success in steeplechase type races and over longer distances. In the Moscow Olympics Budyonny horses featured in the jumping medals (although of course many prominent equestrian nations did not attend that Olympic Games).

Breeding of the Budyonny, which is now extremely prolific throughout Russia on account of its great demand, both at home and abroad, has now spread through most of the south-eastern area of the former Soviet Union.

HEIGHT

15.2-16 h.h.

COLOUR

Predominantly chestnut, some brown and bay, occasionally with bright golden tinge.

HEAD

Full of quality, clean and fine-skinned, showing the Thoroughbred influence.

NECK AND SHOULDERS

Long, straight neck with high withers and adequately sloped shoulder.

BODY

Straight, short back with longish loins and long, straight croup.

LIMBS

Not the best feature of the breed, often rather light in comparison with the body.

Don

Lacking conformational quality and surviving on little to eat, the Don horse was a major factor in the Cossacks' military success.

The Don horse originated in the 18th and 19th centuries as a development from horses of the nomadic tribes of the steppes, influenced by Karabakh, Persian and Turkmene blood. This was the mount of the Don Cossacks, who were instrumental in forcing Napoleon's retreat from Russia during 1812-14. Around that time the breed was improved, using Orlov, Thoroughbred and Strelets Arab blood and the Don remained very much a cavalry horse, having become exceptionally hardy through being forced to survive on the frozen steppes.

HEIGHT

15.3 h.h. average but may be larger, up to 16 h.h.

COLOUR

Chestnut and brown, often with a golden tinge.

CONFORMATION

A big-bodied horse, with a build that is functional rather than athletic. A tendency to various structural defects in the limbs, plus a short, though sloping, shoulder may restrict the action, although the Don's constitutional toughness is unquestioned.

The Don is quite a large horse but, today, it is none the less most valued for its capacity for endurance and long-distance work. In 1950 a group of stallions achieved a record-breaking feat of 305 km (190 miles) in one day, spending twenty hours riding and four hours in rest periods.

Traditionally, the Don is kept in herds on the open steppe and left more or less to fend for itself. The main breeding areas are the south eastern regions of the former USSR, also Kazakhstan and Kirghizia, but the Don is used extensively in other areas as an 'improver' of those breeds kept in free-running herds. The best Don horses are found at the Budyonny and Limovnikovsky Studs in the Rostov region.

Standardbred

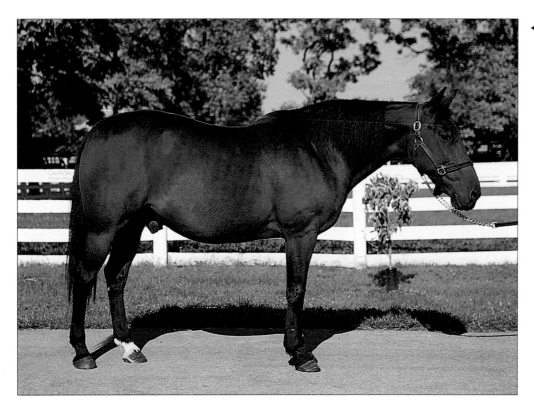

rotting races have captured people's imagination, but the modern sport of harness racing has taken the trotting and pacing horse to its zenith of achievement. At the pinnacle of the trotting breeds is the American Standardbred, capable of trotting 1.6 km (1 mile) against the clock in well under two minutes.

The Standardbred derives from the Narragansett Pacer, a comfortable saddle horse developed in Rhode Island, and the famous grey Thoroughbred Messenger, of the Darley Arabian line, with links to the influential Norfolk Roadster. Messenger was the great-grandsire of Hambletonian, whose prepotency secured the future of the breed, with at least 40 of his offspring able to trot the mile in less than two and a half minutes.

In America, pacers are preferred. Their top speeds are slightly faster than those of trotters but the main reason for the preference is that pacers are raced in 'hobbles', which encourage them to maintain gait, whereas a trotter is more likely to 'break' which results in penalization during the race. In Europe, trotters are more frequently seen, although pacers are gaining ground.

HEIGHT

14-16 h.h.

COLOUR

Usually bay, plus brown, black and chestnut.

HEAD

Honest, with kind expression, if rather plain.

NECK AND SHOULDERS

Neck lean and well-muscled, well set on to powerful shoulders.

BODY

Longish back and exceptionally powerful quarters with the croup often higher than the withers.

LIMBS

Shorter than the Thoroughbred but extremely hard to stand up to the rigours of racing, with good feet.

ACTION

Straight and true; fast, active trot or pace, with immense propulsive power from behind.

SPECIAL SKILLS

Standardbreds have a special lateral pace – the two legs on the same side moving in unison.

French Trotter

In France, every horse has to pass a qualification test for racing. As 50 per cent are rejected selectivity is ensured for improving the breed.

HEIGHT

Around 16.2 h.h.

COLOUR

Chestnut and bay most commonly found.

CONFORMATION

Increasingly following the Thoroughbred but retaining some characteristic Norman traits. The head shows intelligence, though heavier than the Thoroughbred, often with an aquiline profile. The shoulder was originally quite straight but is becoming more slanted to allow a broader movement of the forearm. The overall build is broad, with sound, tough limbs.

*T*ogether with America and Russia, France is one of the great harness-racing nations and has developed its own outstanding trotting breed, which is now claimed to equal the American Standardbred for speed. Like the Selle Français, the French Trotter derives from Thoroughbred and Norman blood but also from the Norfolk Roadster, the English trotting horse that was the progenitor of the Hackney. The Thoroughbred lines of Eclipse, via his great-grandson Phaeton, and Matchem, grandsire of Rattler, are found in French Trotter genealogies. Rattler produced two important lines of descent – through Normand, who was responsible for a dynasty of Selle Français horses, and through Fuschia, a patriarch of the trotter breed.

The statistics of the trotting industry in France are significant. In 1983 over 14,000 'blood' mares were covered by 662 trotter sires. Approximately 9,000 trotters are registered each year and 16,000 horses take part in over 9,000 races. In 1988, 600 million FF in prize money were distributed, averaging 66,000 FF per race at over 280 racetracks. The Vincennes track near Paris is a principal venue, where the 'Prix d'Amerique' is worth 3 million FF. French trotters are raced under saddle as well as in harness, with equally valuable prizes. Most French trotters are owner-trained, making this a highly competitive sport.

Breeding is still concentrated in Normandy, the north west of France, the Loire area and the south west. Despite the size of the sport and the numbers racing, many breeders run small operations with no more than two or three mares, although the stud book is strictly controlled by the French National Stud.

Orlov Trotter

◄ *The Orlov Trotter is one of the many breeds created by the former Soviet Union.*

HEIGHT

15.3-16 h.h.

COLOUR

Predominently grey, also bay, black and chestnut.

HEAD

The relatively small head has a broad forehead and distinctly Arabian features.

NECK AND SHOULDERS

The long, graceful, well-muscled neck rises high out of good shoulders.

BODY

Deep chest and girth, with broad, muscular loins and strong hindquarters.

LIMBS

The best specimens have good bone, sound legs and stand four-square.

ACTION

Elevated, smooth and graceful. The Orlov is in demand as an attractive light-harness horse as well as for the racetrack.

The Orlov Trotter derived from the stallion Bars I, the son of an Arab/Danish stallion and a Dutch mare. Bars I was used at the new Khrenovski Stud, from 1788, at the instigation of Count Orlov, on Arab, Danish and Dutch mares to produce the prototype trotter and the type was further established by careful inbreeding limited to Bars and his sons. Performance-testing on the race track is a feature of most horse-breeding experiments in Russia today and tests for the Orlov began in 1834 in Moscow, which permitted further selectivity to breed for the fastest trotters. Pedigree data were recorded from the start and the first stud book issued in 1847.

The Orlov, however, is not as fast as the trotting supremo, the American Standardbred, and the breed record was set in 1974 by Pion, a grey stallion from the Dubrovsky Stud, which covered 1,600 m (1,750 yd) in 2 minutes 0.1 seconds. The Orlov is undoubtedly Russia's favourite breed, with a population of nearly 50,000 purebreds and over half a million horses of Orlov blood existing in 1980. The Orlov has a long and graceful neck set high on good shoulders, with strong, muscular loins and, overall, well-proportioned conformation, which explains its popularity as an 'improver' to cross with other breeds.

SPECIAL SKILLS

The traditional Russian troika is drawn by three horses. The centre horse trots, while the outer pair canter.

Russian Trotter

The speed of the Russian Trotter is now considered to be on a par with its French and American counterparts. ▶

HEIGHT

Around 16 h.h.

COLOUR

Bay, chestnut, brown, grey.

CONFORMATION

Combining the power and athleticism of the American Standardbred with the elegance of the Orlov Trotter, the Russian Trotter is both durable and attractive. Tough, athletic and agile.

ACTION

Free, swinging trot. Pacing is seldom seen in Russia.

*N*ext to American and France, enthusiasm for trotting races is keenest in Russia. Therefore, when, at the end of the 19th century, it was found that the purpose-bred Orlov lacked the speed of Thoroughbred-based American Standardbreds and French Trotters, there was a strong move to create a speedier animal on the part of a determined group of people who saw this as very necessary. Not unnaturally, it was the Standardbred that the Russian breeders turned to and the Russian Trotter, a Standardbred/Orlov crossbreed, is now bred in various regions, including the Dobrovski Stud in the Ukraine, Gomelski Stud in Byelorussia, Ufa Stud in the Urals and Omsk Stud in Siberia. The breed was formally established in 1949 and a record was set by a stallion named Vlastnyi over 1,600 m (1,750 yd) in 1 minute 58.7 seconds.

Since the early days of the breed in the first part of this century, further out-crosses to American stock have been made to enable the Russian Trotter to compete successfully in international terms. This is the case not only in countries of the former Eastern bloc, but also in countries of the West, such as in Sweden, Norway and West Germany.

American Saddlebred

HEIGHT

Average 15-16 h.h. average.

COLOUR

All are acceptable. Most common are chestnut, bay, brown and black.

HEAD

Large, wide-set eyes; gracefully hooked ears set close together; fine muzzle with large nostrils.

NECK AND SHOULDERS

Long, arched neck, well-flexed at the poll with fine, clean throatlatch and a good amount of space between the jaw-bones. Well-defined withers and deep, sloping shoulders.

BODY

Strong, level back and croup, with tail coming out high.

LIMBS

Front leg set well-forward. Straight legs with broad, flat bones, sharply defined tendons and sloping pasterns.

ACTION

Three or five gaits. Carries itself with a superior air; much presence, quality and style.

The American Saddlebred developed from the now-extinct Narragansett Pacer, a comfortable mount derived from crossing British ponies, imported by the early colonists, with heavier Dutch and French Canadian horses. Further crossings of Thoroughbred, Morgan and Arabian blood produced the Saddlebred, the founding sire of which, the Thoroughbred Denmark, was foaled in 1839. He sired Gaines's Denmark on a naturally gaited mare, and his descendants formed a whole family of Saddlebred horses.

Kentucky was the home of the Saddlebred, which soon spread into Tennessee and Missouri as the favoured mount of plantation owners who needed a comfortable, well-mannered horse from which to oversee their vast estates. The breed registry, the first in America, was formed on 7 April 1891. Soon, rivalry between the states of Kentucky and Missouri led to competition in horse shows and, until the present day, the predominant role of the breed became that of the show horse. Saddlebreds may exhibit either the three usual gaits of walk, trot and canter, or the full five gaits, including the 'slow gait' and the 'rack'. The 'slow gait' is a high-stepping, slow, four-beat pace, while the 'rack' is a spectacular, fast, four-beat gait, not to be confused with pacing.

DISTINGUISHING FEATURES

The high-stepping action of the American Saddlebred is extremely popular with spectators.

Missouri Fox Trotter

The Missouri Fox Trotter shares its history with other American 'gaited' breeds, although its particular gait is unique. ▶

HEIGHT

14-16 h.h.

COLOUR

Various.

HEAD

Neat, clean and intelligent. Pointed ears and large, bright eyes.

NECK AND SHOULDERS

Graceful neck, in proportion and well-joined to the body. Properly sloped and well-muscled shoulders.

BODY

Reasonably short and strong back; deep and well-ribbed body; deep chest.

LIMBS

Muscular and well-tapered with a well-made, strong foot in proportion to the size of horse.

OVERALL IMPRESSION

The animal should stand well on its feet, be erect, wide awake and alert.

The nineteenth-century settlers of Missouri and Kansas needed a tough, easy-to-ride horse that could cover long distances through the Ozark hills without tiring so, like the settlers of Tennesse and Kentucky, they developed their own version of the gaited horse, in this case the Missouri Fox Trotter. Based on Thoroughbred, Morgan and Barb blood, the Fox Trotter is distinctive from the Tennesee Walker and the Saddlebred in that its unique gait comprises walking with the front legs while performing a sliding trot with the hind legs. The result is an extremely smooth movement with no concussion. Saddlebred and Walker blood helped to fix the type and gait, which is rhythmic and can be continued for long periods. The horse also performs a rapid flat-foot walk and a smooth canter.

The Fox Trotter was the 'using horse' of its region, favoured by cattlemen, sheriffs, country doctors and anyone who needed to get from one place to another in relative comfort. Fox Trotters are said to be ideal for children and beginners because of their smooth paces and quiet, willing temperament. No artificial training aids are permitted by the breed association when producing horses for the show ring and the action is lower than that of the Saddlebred and Tennessee Walking Horse, making the Fox Trotter an ideal all-round pleasure horse, with over 39,000 such horses registered in the United States and Canada today.

Tennessee Walking Horse

The distinct gaits of the Tennesse Walking Horse developed from crossing Union trotting horses with Confederate pacers, which produced the smooth-gaited Tennessee pacer. It was found that this policy sometimes produced a horse that showed a new, smooth, four-beat gait that was called a 'running walk'. The first horse noted to possess this tendency was a roan, foaled in 1837 from trotting stock and named Bald Stockings. In 1886, however, the major founding sire of the breed was foaled. By a trotting sire, Allandorf, out of a Morgan mare, Maggie Marshall, the small black stallion named Allan was bred to be a trotter. However, he refused to trot, exhibiting the pace instead. Thus undistinguished, he spent seventeen years being traded from one owner to another until, finally, he was purchased by James Brantley of Tennessee's Coffee County in 1903.

The 15 h.h. stallion was mated to outstanding mares of the area and produced numerous offspring, to whom he passed on his ability to perform the easy, gliding gait known as the running walk. Further selective breeding produced the breed known today as the Tennessee Walking Horse and a Breeders' Association was formed in 1935, although the breed was not officially recognized by the US Department of Agriculture until 1947. The breed has attracted considerable attention as a show horse because of its unique smooth action but it is also used for ranch work, by mounted rangers and for hunting, driving and trail riding.

HEIGHT

15-16 h.h.

COLOUR

Traditional black, or any other solid colour.

CONFORMATION

Strong, square build, short-coupled with powerful quarters and hind limbs. The practice of 'nicking' the tail muscle (illegal in the UK) gives the tail carriage its unnatural height.

ACTION

Highly distinctive, smooth and comfortable, performing a 'flat walk' and 'running walk'. The latter is a four-beat gait which averages around 10-13 kmph (6-8 mph) (faster in the show ring) and is further promoted by shoeing the exceptionally long front feet.

Peruvian Paso

The Peruvian Paso is claimed to guarantee 100 per cent transmission of its gait to all purebred foals. ▶

HEIGHT

14.1-15.2 h.h.

COLOUR

Bay, black, brown, buckskin, chestnut, dun, grey, roan.

HEAD

Medium size with a small muzzle and dark, expressive eyes set well-apart.

NECK

Medium length, gracefully arched. Mane (and tail) abundant with fine, lustrous hair, curly or straight.

BODY

Broad chest; long, well-muscled shoulders, especially at the withers; medium to short back; well-muscled loins and long, wide croup, nicely rounded, with tail set low and carried straight. Barrel deep and underline nearly level from last rib to brisket.

LIMBS

Length of leg and depth of body approximately equal. Straight limbs with medium-length pasterns and short cannons.

The Peruvian Paso is a highly distinctive breed and one of the few remaining naturally gaited breeds of the world. It possesses an arrogant, proud outlook, yet has a docile and gentle nature that certainly stems from its Spanish heritage. Selectively bred in Peru for centuries, the Peruvian Paso's antecedents included the Andalusian, Friesian, Barb and Spanish Jennet, all horses the *conquistadores* imported and depended upon during their conquest of the Inca Empire.

Later, as in the southern states of North America, the owners of the great haciendas needed a comfortable smooth-gaited saddle horse, and the Peruvian Paso met this need. The broken, four-time pace, which is neither diagonal nor lateral as in the pacer, provides a completely smooth ride. It is the pride of Peruvian Paso breeders that these characteristics are completely natural to the breed, due to selective breeding, and are not in anyway forced or artificially 'improved'. If a horse does not display correct action it is considered unsuitable for breeding. Artificial modification or training is positively discouraged.

Recently, the popularity of the breed has gained ground, with horses being exported to the United States, Europe, Australia, the Far East and Canada.

DISTINGUISHING FEATURES

The outward-rolling action of the front limb during extension, known as 'termino' is unique to the Peruvian Paso breed.

Paso Fino

*L*ike the Peruvian Paso, the Paso Fino developed from horses of Andalusian, Barb and Spanish Jennet stock, imported by the *conquistadores*, the latter breed being known in particular for its comfortable gait. This was the gait that was developed, with later additions of other blood, to give the characteristic four-beat gait that gave the Paso Fino its name, *paso fino*, translating as 'fine walk'. Today, the breed is encouraged to move in this gait only under saddle, although the natural gaits can also be executed.

The Paso Fino is born with the ability to perform its special gait, which is an evenly spaced, four-beat lateral gait, with each foot contacting the ground independently in a regular sequence at precise intervals, creating a rapid, unbroken rhythm. Propulsion is primarily from the hind limbs and the motion is absorbed in the back and loins. There are three speeds and varying degrees of collection: the *classic fino* is fully collected, with very short steps, rapid footfall and very slow forward movement; the *paso corto* is executed with medium extension, is more ground covering but unhurried, with moderate forward speed; the *paso largo* is the fastest speed, with longer extension and stride, collection is varied and forward speed depends upon the natural harmony and stride of the individual horse. Two additional gaits which the Paso Fino sometimes performs are the *sobre paso* and the *andadura*.

The movement should be smooth, rhythmic and straight. The horse is elegant and has well-balanced conformation, making it a versatile mount for all types of pleasure riding and showing.

HEIGHT

13.2 -15.2 h.h.

COLOUR

Any, with or without white markings.

CONFORMATION

Bred for its physical balance, with no exaggerated muscling or size in any portion of the horse. Compact in build with long, arched neck flowing into sloping good shoulder. Abundant silky mane and tail. The ideal is dramatic, regal, restrained and generates an aura of presence. It should be elegant with stylish movement.

Cleveland Bay

Queen Elizabeth II is the patron of the Cleveland Bay Horse Society and pure-bred Clevelands are bred at the Royal Stud at Hampton Court. ▶

HEIGHT

16-16.2 h.h.

COLOUR

Bay with black points; grey hairs in mane and tail or small white star permissible.

HEAD

Bold and not too small; eyes large and kindly; ears large and fine.

NECK

Long and lean.

BODY

Wide and deep, with strong back and muscular loins. Shoulders sloping, deep and muscular. Quarters level, powerful and long, with the tail well-set.

LIMBS

Arms and thighs muscular; knees and hocks large; 23 cm (9 in) upwards of good, flat bone. Legs should be as clean and hard as possible.

FEET

One of the most important features of the breed; the feet must be of the best and blue in colour.

ACTION

True, straight and free.

In 1960, only nine purebred Cleveland Bay stallions remained in the UK for breeding. Today, there are approximately 50, but only about 13 purebred filly foals are registered each year and the breed is currently on Category 2 'Endangered', of the Rare Breeds Survival Trust's priority list. The Cleveland is the only horse breed that is native to mainland Britain and it probably dates from Roman times. In the 18th century, the Cleveland was a breed fixed in type – strong and short-legged and capable of carrying great weight. Like the smaller Fell and Dales Ponies, Clevelands were used as pack animals, carrying heavy loads of iron ore from the north Yorkshire mines, and the horses were known as 'Chapmans' – a chapman being a pedlar who carried weighty goods around the countryside.

In the 18th century also, the Cleveland was influenced by some of the best Thoroughbred blood of the time and, a hundred years later, Thoroughbred stallions were also used on Cleveland mares to produce the Yorkshire Coaching Horse – a smart bay much in demand to draw the stylish carriages of the aristocracy. This was the first warning that the Cleveland's usefulness as a cross might actually endanger its survival as a purebred; conversely, its very quality led 19th century farmers to prefer a slower, heavier type of horse, that was easier to keep than the keener Cleveland which required more care and attention.

The Cleveland provides a characteristically striking appearance of quality with size, substance and bone, which is passed on to offspring both pure- and part-bred and it has been used as an improver of stock worldwide.

Irish Draught

HEIGHT

At three years old, stallions 16 h.h. and over, mares 15.2 h.h. and over.

COLOUR

Any strong whole colour, including grey.

HEAD

Head generous and pleasant, not coarse. Bold eyes, set well-apart, wide forehead and long, well-set ears.

NECK

Set on high and carried proudly, showing a good length of rein.

SHOULDERS

Clean-cut and withers well-defined.

BODY

Back strong and girth deep, with strong loins and quarters.

LIMBS

Forearms large and generous, cannon bones short and straight. The upper thighs should be strong and powerful, the second thighs well-developed, the hocks sound and generous.

HOOVES

Hard and sound.

ACTION

Smooth, straight and free, without exaggeration, but with good flexing of the hocks.

*T*he Irish Draught could be described as a breed for the modern day – in the sense that its origins are obscure, but its value as the progenitor of athletic, but equable, hunters and competition horses for show jumping and eventing is unrivalled. It was the all-purpose farm and riding horse of rural Ireland, probably deriving from the crossing of indigenous mares with imported Thoroughbred stallions. The mares, in their turn, had almost certainly developed from the Connemara Pony, deriving their size, when bred on Ireland's perfect horse-raising pastures, from the Spanish and Arabian blood that had long before influenced the pony breed of Ireland's rugged western coast.

The Andalusian influence is easily detected in the modern Irish Draught, in its proud carriage and appearance of substance with quality. Although technically a 'draught' breed, it is light of feather and its conformation, with a good shoulder and free, active action, readily lends itself to ridden rather than to harness work. Of course, along with many other breeds, the Irish Draught suffered a huge decline in numbers with the advent of mechanization and it was not until 1976 that the Irish Draught Horse Society was formed, followed in 1979 by the Irish Draught Horse Society (Great Britain).

Numbers are still small, a principal problem being the demand for half-bred Irish Draughts for hunting and show jumping, which has proved more profitable for breeders than maintaining the pool of purebred foundation stock, thus encouraging them to send purebred mares to Thoroughbred stallions.

Dutch Gelderlander

A typical example of the remarkably 'true to type' Dutch Gelderlander. ►

HEIGHT

15.2-16.2 h.h.

COLOUR

Predominantly chestnut, often with some white on the legs, some grey and very rarely skewbald.

HEAD

Carried high, long face with calm expression.

NECK AND SHOULDERS

Strong neck rising from well-set, sloping shoulders.

BODY

Fairly long back, deep girth. Straight croup with high-set tail and powerful quarters.

LIMBS

Short, well-made, clean and very strong.

ACTION

Stylish and rhythmic action with more freedom than most light draught breeds, giving suitability for riding as well as driving.

A team of Dutch Gelderlander horses in harness, heads held high, is an impressive sight. Even more impressive is a show ring filled with fast, high-stepping teams competing in a turnout class in their native Netherlands, where driving is a highly popular equestrian sport. The flat Dutch countryside, with its wide forest and farmland tracks, is ideally suited to carriage driving for sport, the problem in many other countries being finding somewhere suitable to practise!

These bright chestnut horses, usually with white blazes and often with white extending well up the legs, are easy to match and, although they appear rather plain out of harness, there are no finer horses once put to the task for which they were bred. The Gelderlander was developed by breeders in the central Netherlands province of Gelder, from which they took their name. It is a modern breed, not much more than a hundred years old, which was bred up from native mares, principally by adding Thoroughbred and Holstein blood but also using a wide cross-section of other breeds, including some from eastern Europe. The type eventually produced was further adjusted with touches of Oldenburg, East Friesian, Hackney and Anglo Norman, so the Gelderlander is a truly cosmopolitan breed, although, perhaps surprisingly, homogenous in type. Its appeal is as universal as its origins and it is widely exported, being much in demand as a driving competition horse.

Normandy Cob

The horses of France tend to be very distinctive in type – the result of a precisely controlled breeding programme aimed at producing 'horses for courses', and the Normandy Cob is no exception, unlike the familiar English-cum-Irish Cob, the breeding of which is usually accidental rather than planned. However, the two have similar attributes, except that the Normandy Cob can reach a greater height than the English.

Acknowledged as a 'half-breed', the Normandy Cob was developed as a dual-purpose horse, to be both ridden and used for agricultural and light draught work in the Manche region. It is now, however, centred on the Saint-Lo National Stud.

There were formerly two types of Normandy Cob. The lighter, closer to the Thoroughbred in type, though with a deep chest and short legs, was superseded by the saddle horses that became the preferred riding horses of France. There remains a heavier type, now a smart harness horse and still used for field work in the arable lands of Normandy.

SHOW PRESENTATION

The 'docking' of horses' tails is now banned in Great Britain and a neatly pulled tail shows off the strong, rounded quarters of the show cob to advantage.

HEIGHT

15.3-16.3 h.h.

COLOUR

Bay or chestnut with occasional red roan or grey.

CONFORMATION

Head and general features resemble a heavy Norman saddle horse. Rather cubic in shape, with good limbs, close to the ground and strong; harmonious and well-balanced.

ACTION

Energetic, with good gaits.

DUAL-PURPOSE SADDLE/LIGHT HARNESS HORSES

Hackney Horse/Pony

The modern Hackney, harnessed to a light, four-wheeled 'show wagon', appears to float over the ground. ▶

HEIGHT

Ponies 14 h.h. and under; horses over 14 h.h.

COLOUR

Usually bay, dark brown, chestnut or black.

HEAD

Small and convex with large eyes; small ears and muzzle.

NECK

Long and well-formed.

SHOULDERS

Powerful with low withers.

BODY

Compact with great depth of chest. Tail well set on to quarters and carried high.

LIMBS

Forelegs straight; gentle slope to pastern and well-shaped feet. Strong, well-let-down hocks.

ACTION

Brilliance and correctness of action is paramount. The head erect, neither too high nor low, the ears pricked and the whole animal a portrait of elegance and beauty.

Today the Hackney is more likely to be found in the show ring, where driving and *concours d'élégance* classes contribute a thrilling spectacle, than in its former working role. Historically, the Hackney Horse and Pony both originated in the north and east of England, being derivatives of the old Norfolk Roadster, Yorkshire Trotter and, in the case of the Hackney Pony, the Fell Pony. Both the Norfolk Roadster and Yorkshire Trotter can be traced back, via a horse called Original Shales, to the Darley Arabian. Original Shales, foaled in 1755, was by Blaze out of a trotting mare.

These trotting horses used to cover great distances – 80-90 km (50-60 miles) in a day taking farmer-owners to market and back was commonplace – and their brilliant, high-stepping action soon created a demand for them among the higher social classes, for transport, for crossing with other breeds to produce officers' chargers for the army and for export. Matching pairs were required to put to the carriages of the aristocracy. There are many recorded instances of Hackneys covering 25 km (16 miles) in an hour, carrying 38 kg (12 stone) in weight, but one particular feat worth mentioning is that of a mare, Nonpareil, who reputedly trotted 161 km (100 miles) in nine hours 56 minutes, with no ill effects.

SPECIAL SKILLS

The extremely elevated knee action of the Hackney makes it the ultimate, elegant harness horse.

Morgan

◀ *The high head carriage of the Morgan is similar to that of the Welsh Cob.*

HEIGHT

14.1-15.2 h.h.

COLOUR

Predominantly bay, plus chestnut, brown and black. Occasionally grey, buckskin or palomino.

HEAD

Expressive, with broad forehead, large, prominent eyes and straight or slightly dished, short face. Ears should be short, set rather wide apart and carried alertly. The gullet is a little deeper than in other breeds and refined sufficiently to allow proper flexion at the poll.

NECK AND SHOULDER

The neck should rise from a well-angulated shoulder and be slightly arched and blend with the withers and back.

BODY

Compact with a short back, close-coupled, broad loins, deep flank, well-sprung ribs, croup long and well-muscled, with tail attached high and carried straight.

LIMBS

Straight and sound with short cannons and flat bone. Forearm long and the pasterns long and sloping.

ACTION

The walk should be rapid and elastic with a four-beat cadence; the trot should be two-beat, animated and collected; the canter smooth and balanced.

There is no breed of more romantic appeal than the Morgan horse. Its origins, so mysterious that even its name belongs to that of the man who owned it – Justin Morgan, a tavern keeper – give rise to a host of speculations. The romance continues – its extraordinary prepotency, which can only be termed freakish, its longevity, its proud and regal carriage, contrasting with a gentle, willing and hard-working nature, its elegant and refined conformation, combined with renowned stamina and endurance, all give the Morgan its own special magic.

Justin Morgan was foaled around 1790 and was said to be by a horse called True Briton, who may have been a Thoroughbred but was more likely a Welsh Cob. He was a small horse, just 14 h.h. and dark bay, with a black mane, tail and legs. During his life he was often put to the test in racing and weight-pulling contests.

The first Morgan horse register was published in 1894, the US Morgan Horse Farm was established in Vermont in 1907 and the Morgan Horse Club was formed in 1909, becoming the American Morgan Horse Association in 1971. Today, the Morgan is a versatile breed, retaining all the characteristics of its founding sire. Two types evolved: the pleasure horse, used for jumping, dressage and endurance as well as the full range of Western equitation classes; and the park horse, which has a more animated, high-stepping trot and is the picture of refined elegance.

Lipizzaner

The Lipizzaner is equally at home as the spirited haute ecole performer or as the prosaic plough horse. ▶

HEIGHT

Ideally from 15-16 h.h.

COLOUR

Predominantly white, although other colours do occur.

HEAD

Lean and large, often with a 'broken' nose line. Ears large and eyes intelligent.

NECK

Muscular and high set.

SHOULDERS

Often short and steep.

BODY

The chest is broad and deep, but not especially pronounced. The back is often long, but always strong and the loins are long, rounded and muscular. The tail is set high and well-carried.

LIMBS

Tend to be short; medium-length cannons and wide, well-defined joints, with short, elastic pasterns. The hooves are small and tough.

ACTION

High and energetic.

Every serious horse lover has heard of the white stallions of Vienna, the Lipizzaners of the famous Spanish Riding School, which perform the 'airs above the ground' which are the epitome of 'haute ecole', together with the dancing movements of classical equitation.

The Spanish Riding School derives its name from the Spanish blood of the Andalusian horses that formed the basis of the Lipizzaner breed, which, in turn. takes its name from the stud created in 1580 by Archduke Charles II of Austria at Lipizza, near Trieste. Here, nine stallions and 24 mares formed the foundation stock of the breed which later developed six distinct lines named after their founding stallions – Conversano, a black Neapolitan; Favory, a dun from the Austrian stud at Kladrub; Maestoso, a white horse also from Kladrub; Siglavy, a white desert Arab; Pluto, a white horse of pure Spanish descent; and Neopolitano, a bay Neapolitan. The Spanish Riding School horses are bred at Piber, in former Yugoslavia.

Apart from their fame as high school horses, Lipizzaners are very successful in competitive driving, particularly in Hungary, and have been produced to international level. Over time, grey has become the predominant colour, with dun, cream, brown and palomino colouring gradually disappearing. An occasional bay is found and the Spanish Riding School always has one bay horse among its performers. Foals are born black or brown and acquire their white coats gradually as they mature.

Shagya Arabian

Few breeds have a more romantic history than that of the Shagya Arab, the best known of the Hungarian breeds, sometimes also referred to as the Hungarian Shagya. Established at the picturesque stud of Ba'bolna, near Budapest, when Hungarian horse-breeding was at its height in the early 19th century, the Shagya was specifically bred as a light cavalry horse, using purebred desert Arabian stallions on local Hungarian mares of oriental type. The breed was named Shagya, after a single stallion which was imported from Syria in 1836, to distinguish the breed from the pure Arabians bred at Ba'bolna. Careful line-breeding fixed the type and resulted in a superb saddle horse.

During the First World War, many horses were evacuated to Austria, although a number were seized by Rumania. The Second World War caused further depredations, with most of the horses left scattered in Austria, Germany, Poland and even America. Reconstruction led to the present-day population which includes 60 Shagya mares, but the breed is still recovering from a further misguided policy of diluting the old bloodlines with too much Egyptian Arabian blood. Fortunately, Ba'bolna has been able to reintroduce the influence of lines that had been exported to Germany and Switzerland and thus revive the true-to-type Shagya.

Today, the Shagya is a valuable endurance and pleasure horse, also good in harness, rather than the mount of the hussar. The statue at the gates of Ba'bolna of a rider-less stallion who returned to the stud during the Napoleonic wars is a potent reminder of its brave past in the service of its country.

HEIGHT

14.1-15 h.h.

COLOUR

Predominantly grey.

HEAD

Dished profile, small, tapered muzzle and very large eyes.

CONFORMATION

The Shagya has the outline and beautifully refined head of the Arabian, coupled with a more powerful skeletal structure, giving extra size, substance and bone. The shoulder is sloping, withers prominent, back short, tail carriage high. The limbs are strong and correct, with at least 19 cm (7½ in) of bone; feet tough and well-shaped.

ACTION

Free and springing off the ground.

Nonius

HEIGHT

Large Nonius 15.3-16.2 h.h.
Small Nonius 14.3-15.3 h.h.

COLOUR

Usually bay, occasionally brown, black or chestnut.

CONFORMATION

Large Nonius: basically half-bred type, tending towards carriage-horse conformation, well-proportioned with comparatively short limbs and plenty of good bone. Late maturing, but long-lived. Small Nonius: similar to large Nonius, but finer and more of a 'riding' type.

ACTION

Free, active paces.

Hungary is a country of horse breeders – the equine heritage of these originally nomadic people is exceptionally strong and has resulted in the evolution of four distinct national breeds, the Shagya Arab, the Gidran (an Arab cross), the Nonius and the Furioso. During the 19th century, Hungary was the army remount centre of Europe, producing horses for many countries, including Britain, and the national horse herd population exceeded two million.

The Nonius is best described as a middleweight carriage horse, although there is a smaller type which is an active riding horse. The breed was based on one stallion, Nonius Senior, which was captured by the Hungarian cavalry which defeated Napoleon at Leipzig in 1813. Nonius Senior was an Anglo Norman horse of questionable beauty but he was a prolific sire who threw excellent stock and produced fifteen sons for the furtherance of the new breed. The original Nonius was bred as mainly a light agricultural horse. Nowadays the purebred is used in competitive driving events, which are extremely popular in Hungary.

The Nonius was first bred at the famous Mezohegyes Stud, which had been founded by Emperor Joseph II in 1785, the era of the Austro-Hungarian Empire's greatest power. In more recent, less romantic times, Mezohegyes, along with the rest of Hungary's equine heritage, was taken over by the Communist regime and became a state stud. The departure of the Soviets, at the beginning of the 1990s, however, heralded a new era for Hungarian horse breeding, which is enjoying a period of renewed vigour.

Furioso

The Furioso was a further development of the Nonius breed at the Mezohegyes Stud in Hungary and is the equivalent of the modern west European Warmblood. It carries the Anglo Norman blood of the Nonius, further refined by more Thoroughbred blood, to give a more athletic, but still substantial, conformation.

The Furioso takes its name from one of the two founding sires, Furioso, a Thoroughbred imported into Hungary around 1840. The other, also a Thoroughbred, was North Star, imported a few years later. North Star was the grandson of Waxy, which won the Derby in 1793, and he also had strong trotting and roadster links. The two lines were originally kept separate, Furioso siring no less than 95 stallions which were sent to many of the Austro-Hungarian Empire's studs. Later on, the Thoroughbred influence was reintroduced and eventually the two lines were mixed, with the Furioso strain becoming dominant.

Despite its strongly Thoroughbred heritage, seen clearly in the head, the Furioso very much retains the overall appearance of a light carriage horse, the limbs and action especially tending towards that type. It is a useful harness horse, but also a good all-round competitor, often taking part in cross-country jumping.

HEIGHT

Average 16 h.h. plus.

COLOUR

Usually solid black, dark brown or bay. White markings are rare.

CONFORMATION

Intelligent head, with squarer muzzle and larger ears than the Thoroughbred. Upstanding appearance, with Thoroughbred refinement over-lying coaching-horse origins. 'Riding' shoulder and withers but croup sloping, though powerful, with strong limbs and well-defined joints.

ACTION

Active movement, with more height than is required in a competition horse.

Norwegian Fjord

The pony-sized Fjord is an excellent example of equine versatility. ▶

HEIGHT

13-14.2 h.h.

COLOUR

Various shades of dun, with dorsal (eel) stripe and zebra markings on the legs. Mane hair consists of black hairs in the centre and cream or blonde hairs on the outside; the tail is a mixture of dark and cream or blonde hairs. No white markings permissible except a small star on the forehead.

HEAD

The face may be dished with a flat forehead; ears small; eyes set wide apart. The neck may be strong and crested.

BODY

Short-coupled and compact, with deep chest and girth. Sturdy and muscular.

LIMBS

Strong, clean legs with short cannons.

ACTION

Flowing and free, sometimes extravagant.

The Norwegian Fjord retains more of the characteristics of the primitive *Equus przewalskii przewalskii poliakov*, the Asiatic Wild Horse, than any other breed, particularly in terms of colour, a shade of golden dun, and markings, which include the dorsal stripe and zebra markings on the legs. In Scandinavia the Fjord is known as 'the Yellow Horse'.

In its native territory, where it thrived in the inhospitable climate of the Norwegian fjords and was very economical to keep, the Fjord's principal role was as a workhorse, capable of pulling heavy loads for its size. Upbreeding produced a taller Fjord but then, during the Second World War, the German army demanded smaller Fjords to use as pack horses. Today, larger Fjords, up to 14.2 h.h., may be found once more.

Selection procedures for breeding stock are very strict, with the result that the Fjord has remained extremely hardy and strong, with excellent limbs, bone and feet. An ideal all-purpose family mount, with an exceptionally willing temperament, the Fjord's particular *métier* is as a harness horse and the breed has been very successful in driving competitions.

DISTINGUISHING FEATURES

The Fjord horse's mane is trimmed into a crescent shape, with the dark centre hairs standing proud of the blond outer hairs.

Haflinger

◄ *The appealing Haflinger is exceptionally strong for its size.*

*T*he Haflinger is undoubtedly one of the most attractive of the world's pony breeds, with its deep chestnut coat and its abundant, flowing, flaxen mane and tail. Although various shades of chestnut are permitted, no other colour is ever allowed and the purity of colour of the mane and tail, the breed's most marked and distinguished characteristics, is strictly adhered to.

The Haflinger hails from the mountains of Austria and is descended from the extinct Alpine Heavy Horse and other native Tyrolean breeds, all with a similar genetic background, plus a single Arabian stallion, El Bedavi XXII, to which all modern Haflingers trace their heritage. This Arabian connection, introduced after the wars against the Turks, contributed spirit and elegance to the breed, which makes it a lively and exceptionally versatile ridden pony as well as a small draught horse. All ponies bred at Hafling, the mountain village from which the pony takes its name, carry a brand of the edelweiss – Austria's national flower – with an 'H' at the centre. Although hardy, Haflingers do not tolerate a combination of cold and wet weather and in their native country they are kept in the time-honoured way in stables beneath the farmhouse. They are natural driving ponies, being both strong and easily manoeuvrable.

The Haflinger excels at endurance events, both ridden and driven, and makes an active show jumper. Its kind temperament makes it particularly suitable for work with the Riding for the Disabled Association in Great Britain and it has been exported worldwide.

HEIGHT

13.1-14.3 h.h.

COLOUR

Chestnut – light, middle, liver or red; mane and tail flaxen. White star or stripe permitted; white on legs or body discouraged.

HEAD

Short with slight dish. Large, dark and lively eyes, fine nostrils and small, pliable ears.

NECK

Strong and well-positioned, not too short.

BODY

Broad, deep chest, well-muscled back, broad loins, a muscular croup that is not too short and a well-carried tail. Deep girth, measuring 165-190 cm (65-75 in).

LIMBS

Clean, with hard, healthy hooves. Strong forearms and a good second thigh; short cannons with plenty of bone.

Brumby

*H*orses are not indigenous to Australia and were first imported in 1788 by the early settlers. Some came from India and some from Chile but most came from the Cape of Good Hope and were of Arab and Barb stock. As time went on, Thoroughbreds were imported to improve the riding stock, Clydesdales for draught work and Cleveland Bays for carriages. From a few of these early horses, which escaped from the settlers' camps in the days of the Australian gold rush, the ubiquitous Brumby developed. Quickly turning feral and without natural enemies, the horses bred rapidly and indiscriminately, at the same time degenerating in quality, due to inbreeding and the hard conditions of the outback in which they lived. Tough and cunning, with the whole outback in which to hide, the Brumbies were almost impossible to catch and, when caught, considered almost impossible to tame.

Remarkably, the situation continued unabated until the 1960s, when around 8,000 wild horses were estimated to be roaming to the west of Brisbane and a concerted effort was made to catch them for slaughter, using planes and jeeps. Since then, the method of culling using helicopters and high-powered rifles has roused universal outrage, with the horse world shocked at such an inhumane and uncertain method of hunting and slaughter, while the authorities maintain that the effect of drought and famine on so many animals is a worse fate.

HEIGHT

None specified, but tending towards small, scrub stock.

COLOUR

Any.

CONFORMATION

Degenerated due to inbreeding and harsh environment.

Mustang

The Mustang of America, like the Brumby of Australia, developed from domesticated horses that had either escaped or been turned loose. The word 'mustang' derives from either, or both, of two Spanish words – *mesteno*, referring to an association of graziers, and *mostrenco*, which means a homeless stray.

The Mustangs themselves were the descendants of the original Spanish horses, brought to the New World by the *conquistadores*, and, despite centuries of indiscriminate breeding and surviving on what they could glean from the Mexican and North American wilderness, their Spanish origins are still apparent. The wild herds increased rapidly and, by the beginning of the 20th century, it was estimated that over a million horses were at liberty in the American west. During the early 1900s, the Mustangs were severely persecuted, being rounded up and slaughtered for meat and hides. The Mustang was supposed to be ill-tempered when tamed, but this undoubtedly had more to do with the rough methods of the cowboys who set out to master the wild horses than to their natural inclination.

By the late 1960s, the Mustang population had dwindled to a very low level of around 17,000 and the preservation of America's wild horse, together with a backlash of public opinion against the wholesale and apparently senseless slaughter, became a government issue. Today the Mustang is protected by law. Although numbers are controlled, the quality has improved very greatly and the well-broken Mustang makes a useful all-round cow pony. It is a very hardy animal and capable of surviving on very little food.

HEIGHT

Around 13.2-15 h.h.

COLOUR

Any.

CONFORMATION

The original Mustangs were robust, sturdy horses, often heavy in the head and not very attractive. They had particularly hard, sound legs and feet, enabling them to cope unshod in rough terrain. Today, as part of the preservation effort, animals with improved conformation and appearance are being bred and new individual strains, such as the Cayuse Indian Pony and the Rocky Mountain Pony, have now appeared.

Pinto

HEIGHT

Between 14-17 h.h.

COLOUR

The Overo has a dark background with white patches, while the Tobiano's background is white with dark patches.

CONFORMATION

Four types of Pinto Horse are recognized by the Pinto Horse Association:

1. Stock Type: horses of predominantly Quarter Horse breeding with the original Shetland used to produce ponies.

2. Hunter Type: horses of predominantly Thoroughbred breeding with the introduction of the Connemara to produce ponies.

3. Pleasure Type: horses of Arabian or Morgan origin with the Welsh Pony introduced to produce smaller animals.

4. Saddle Type: horses bred from the Saddlebred, Hackney or Tennessee Walking Horse with the introduction of the American Shetland to produce ponies.

Whether called Pinto, paint, or just coloured horse, broken-coloured horses, like spotted horses, have been prized – or despised – by various cultures of the world since time immemorial, but nowhere was the coloured horse allotted such a heritage as in the United States, particularly among the American Indians. The Indians were eminently practical and soon recognized the advantage, for camouflage purposes, of a broken-coloured horse in open country. The coloured horse was also supposed to have magical properties, which would protect its rider in battle. The ceremonially dressed 'paint' horse, with an Indian rider in tribal costume, is a striking sight in parades today and it is only in America that the coloured horse has been given breed status, having been bred in sufficient numbers to have its own designation, although one or two societies do promote coloured horses in other countries.

Like most American breeds, the Pinto derives from Spanish origins and there are two colour types. Overo describes a dark-coloured background with splashes of white which do not spread over the back and tail. The Tobiano is mainly white, usually including all four legs, with dark splashes on the body; the head is often dark, with white markings. The Pinto Horse Association of America was formed in 1956 and horses take part in races and the whole range of Western riding events – barrel racing, roping, reining, etc. – as well as English-style events.

Palomino

◄ *Although colour is the basis of the Palomino, breeders are also concerned to breed for quality and good conformation.*

he Palomino is not a breed, but a colour type, that has become as distinctive as an individual breed because of the great value and esteem placed on this particular colour: golden with a white mane and tail. Both Great Britain and America have associations to promote the Palomino, but with differing regulations. For example, the American association requires one Palomino parent, with the other having Arabian, Quarter Horse or Thoroughbred bloodlines, for a horse to be eligible for registration. The British association permits registration of horses and ponies from any recognized stud book in their pedigree register and has a second register for animals from parents of unregistered or unknown breeding.

The palomino colour does not occur in purebred Arabians or Thoroughbreds, but selective breeding for colour has resulted in many Palomino horses of Thoroughbred and, more particularly, Arabian type. It is frequently found in the larger Welsh breeds and in the American Saddlebred as well as the Quarter Horse. Historically, Queen Isabella of Spain encouraged the breeding of Palominos and they were once referred to as 'Golden Isabellas'.

Obtaining the colour is no easy matter – Palomino to Palomino might produce a chestnut or cremello offspring instead of another Palomino; chestnut to Palomino will produce either chestnut or Palomino, but if it gives Palomino it will be a rich colour; grey to Palomino is most likely to produce another grey, even though the foal may be born Palomino. Although colour is the basis of registration, breeders are also concerned to breed quality and good conformation into their stock.

HEIGHT

Any.

COLOUR

Ideally like a newly minted gold coin, but three shades lighter or darker are acceptable. White markings only on legs and face. Mane and tail white with no more than 15 per cent dark or chestnut hairs. Eyes dark brown, hazel or black iris. Skin dark except under white facial markings.

CONFORMATION AND ACTION

Varies according to type or breed.

Hunter

The hunter, as its name suggests, developed as the horse of the chase. It is, of course, a 'type', not being of any particular breed, but usually a combination of Thoroughbred and something else, often Irish Draught. Its first use is in hunting and its second, derived from the first, is in show hunter classes, which are the foundation of the British summer show scene.

It is unfortunate that show ring fashions have dictated that the animal produced for showing must be so perfect in presentation that blemishes acquired through honest hunting use are frowned upon. Luckily, however, the trend towards overweight show hunters has been recognized to be damaging to the horse.

Many cross-breeds are used to produce hunters, which for showing are divided into three weight classes, plus divisions for small hunters and ladies' hunters. The lightweight hunter will have a large percentage of Thoroughbred blood and is expected to be an upstanding, elegant horse; the middleweight must be capable of carrying up to 89 kg (14 stone) all day in the hunting field and is therefore more substantial but should still show quality and refinement; the true heavyweight, carrying up to more than 89 kg (14 stone), yet still a powerful and athletic jumper, is a difficult horse to find today.

HEIGHT

15-17 h.h. plus.

COLOUR

Any permitted, but solid colours preferred, including grey.

CONFORMATION

A riding horse of substance, with clean, sound limbs and good bone.

ACTION

Straight, true and free, with the minimum of knee action.

SPECIAL SKILLS

The ability to gallop well is an essential characteristic of the modern show hunter.

Hack

*H*ack, the original term for an ordinary riding horse, also means a person for hire who is overworked and has the same language derivation as the word 'hackney', also thought to be connected with the French *haquenée*, meaning 'ambling horse'. Today, however, the words hack and hackney denote two quite different sorts of horse. The hack, a type, not a breed, refers to the elegant show horse that is the descendant of the traditional riding horse, used for everyday transport.

The modern show hack may be anything from a Thoroughbred ex-racehorse to a refined Anglo or part-bred Arab, carefully bred and produced for the job. The principal requirement is a horse of supremely refined elegance and correct conformation – a horse, in fact, designed to complement and enhance the appearance of the lady or gentleman mounted upon it. The other requirement is that the horse should exhibit perfect manners and be schooled to a high degree of obedience. The combination of this requirement with high breeding can be difficult to achieve as the breeds used are the most hot-blooded, sensitive and volatile. The perfect show hack is one of the most challenging creatures to produce but, enjoying its work and ridden side-saddle in the summer sunshine, it creates a most elegant equestrian scene.

SHOW PRESENTATION

In show classes for ladies' hacks, the horses are ridden side saddle which looks very elegant.

HEIGHT

Small exceeding 14.2 h.h. but not over 15 h.h.; large exceeding 15 h.h. but not over 15.3 h.h.

COLOUR

Any permitted, but solid colours preferred, including grey. White markings on face and legs permitted.

CONFORMATION

A lightweight riding horse of refined build, with fine but dense, good-quality bone. Clean-cut head carried on a long, graceful neck flowing into an excellent sloping shoulder.

ACTION

Long, low, straight, balanced and true.

Cob

HEIGHT

15.1 h.h. maximum.

COLOUR

Any colour, including piebald and skewbald.

CONFORMATION

The distinguishing features of the cob are short legs with good quality but solid bone, a powerful, broad physique with a short back and bulky muscles. Despite its thickset build, the cob must not be coarse in appearance, but rather intelligent and workmanlike.

ACTION

Straight and powerful, with some elevation.

The cob has been called the honest broker of the horse world. In the 20th century, throughout the last century, and for who knows how long before that, wherever there was work to be done, there the cob would be found. Very definitely a type and not a breed, there is no apparent genetic predisposition to assist in the breeding of cobs, except that somewhere in the make-up there will be draught-horse breeding to some degree and there is also likely to be Thoroughbred. The parentage is frequently of Irish blood, although it may include Shire, Welsh Cob or any other harness breed.

In former days, the cob might have carried the local doctor or clergyman or taken a farmer to market with a laden trap or out for a day with the hunt. For neatness, the mane is always hogged for showing and, until the practice was prohibited by law in Great Britain in 1948, the tail would have been docked (partially amputated), with the excuse that it was thus kept out of the way when the horse was working in harness. In truth, this was done for the sake of appearance and was most cruel, not only because of the pain inflicted, but also because it robbed the horse of any means of flicking away flies.

The modern cob works mainly in the hunting field and is immensely popular in the show ring, where it is shown either as a lightweight (carrying up to 89 kg or 14 stone) or heavyweight (over 89 kg or 14 stone).

Riding Horse

◄ '*Riding Horse' is a modern definition for show purposes of the good all-round saddle horse.*

*R*iding horse classes are a relatively new addition to the traditional showing classes of the British show ring and they reflect the need to find a niche for the horse that is less substantial than the hunter, less refined than the hack, less robust than the cob and yet is a good-looking, general-purpose horse and a pleasure to ride – an upmarket version, in fact, of the type of horse that thousands of leisure riders own and enjoy.

It is, of course, a type and is usually half-bred, or part-bred, that is, a mixture of Thoroughbred and any combination of other native breeds, which may or may not also include Arab. Frequently, the precise breeding details of such horses are unrecorded but the type is perpetuated by owners who breed from their much-loved mares for the fun and pleasure of breeding their own foal. The results, of course, vary from excellent to disastrous, depending upon the quality of the mare and the appropriate, or inappropriate, choice of sire.

The show riding horse must have correct conformation, good straight action and present an efficient, attractive picture. It must be well-mannered, calm and obedient and capable of performing all the paces well.

HEIGHT

Around 15.2 h.h.

COLOUR

Any permitted.

CONFORMATION

Medium build with well set on head and neck. Good shoulder, sloping at 45 degrees. Limbs four-square and straight, short cannons, medium-sloping pasterns, hocks well let down.

ACTION

Straight, economical and balanced, showing a good length of stride.

TYPES OF SHOW AND SPORT HORSE

Children's Riding Pony

$\mathcal{T}$he children's riding pony is the star of the British show ring; as petite and dainty as a fairy, like a picture from the top of a chocolate box. Breeding show ponies is a highly competitive business and classes are often huge, with the competition to qualify for the major shows and awards nail-bitingly intense. The ponies are shown in their height sizes, ridden by young 'jockeys', the best of whom are as professional and determined as any seasoned adult showpeople. The best child riders are very much in demand and many ponies are produced professionally by experts, rather than by owner/exhibitors. For all that, many families gain a great deal of fun from buying, training and exhibiting their own ponies.

The riding pony, like the bigger show animals, is a type, not a breed, and today is really a mini-Thoroughbred. Pure- and part-bred Welsh Section B ponies are also found; some have a touch of Arabian blood and others a touch of various breeds of native pony, but only enough to give a 'pony' stamp and never enough to detract from the refined appearance that is essential for success. Apart from the three weight classes, smaller ponies may be shown as first ridden, or leading rein ponies.

HEIGHT

12.2 h.h. and under; 13.2 h.h. and under; 14.2 h.h. and under.

COLOUR

Solid colours preferred, including grey.

CONFORMATION

Correct riding conformation with small, pretty head, graceful neck and sloping shoulder. Overall appearance dainty and extremely elegant.

ACTION

Low, 'daisy cutting', and straight, with the hocks moving well underneath the body.

SHOW PRESENTATION

Turnout is critical in show pony classes. Manes and tails are neatly plaited, hooves are oiled, coats polished and the skin round eyes and nostrils accentuated with a fine smear of baby oil. The young riders' turnout must also be immaculate.

Polo Pony

Although it is always called a pony, no height limit is set today for the equine used in the fast and furious game of polo. However, the type has evolved to a high degree, the definitive polo pony now being regarded as the one developed in Argentina where mastery of the sport reaches its height.

Polo was a popular game during the British occupation of India and at that time some Indian breeds were used. Arabs have also played their part but it is the combination of the English Thoroughbred and the Criollo, the native mount of the Argentinian *gaucho*, which has come to the fore. The best polo ponies are usually about threequarter Thoroughbred and one-quarter Criollo, thus giving pony toughness and agility to Thoroughbred speed and stamina. The polo pony must be brave, spirited but calm, have quick acceleration yet be able to stop and turn in an instant. Even though the chukkas, or periods of play into which the game is divided, last only a few minutes and the pony is changed for a fresh one at the end of each chukka, polo is played at the gallop and is extremely demanding on the pony, so tough limbs and feet and a sound, hardy constitution are essential. Argentinian polo ponies are said to have an inbred talent for the game.

SHOW PRESENTATION

The fast and furious game of polo can be dangerous. The ponies' legs are well-bandaged to below the fetlock and the players also wear protective knee pads.

HEIGHT

Not specified, but usually around 15.1 h.h.

COLOUR

Any.

CONFORMATION

Built for agile movement. Well set on head with good flexion, neck relatively long but not heavy; strong shoulders with prominent withers, a short back, well-sprung ribs, muscular, powerful quarters and well let down, strong hocks. The mane is hogged to avoid tangling with the stick.

ACTION

Flexible and supple – able to 'turn on a sixpence'.

TYPES OF SHOW AND SPORT HORSE

British Sport Horse

Only recently has an attempt been made to begin to quantify and record Britain's valuable pool of cross-bred competition horses. ▶

HEIGHT

15-17 h.h.

COLOUR

Any.

CONFORMATION

Varies according to purpose and crossing breeds but always athletic with well-angulated joints and ample room for muscle attachment. Short cannons, well let down hocks, good bone and well-shaped feet.

ACTION

Active and straight, with a good length of stride.

For some time various European countries have developed Warmblood horses to compete in various equestrian disciplines, but there is also a wealth of British cross-bred competition horse stock which can broadly be termed the British Sport Horse.

A number of breeds are involved in the production of sport horses, which are destined for dressage, horse trials and show jumping. The basis for all, however, is the Thoroughbred. In horse trials, many straight Thoroughbreds are successful. However, a touch of something else – an eighth or a sixteenth – is valued as contributing hardiness and a sense of self-preservation. The Irish Draught is the breed most favoured as the foundation cross, such horses possessing substance, power, athleticism and an equable temperament. The Cleveland Bay is less frequently found but can contribute native toughness and good feet and limbs, while the Welsh Cob produces an exceptionally bold and athletic cross and size is seldom lost in the transition. Arab blood also occurs, more frequently than is admitted, and a small percentage can only add to the quality, stamina and soundness of the final result. A limited amount of heavy horse blood, such as Shire or Suffolk, can give power to show jumping horses, provided quality and athleticism are not sacrificed.

The ideal British bred dressage horse is harder to find as current fashion favours the Warmblood which has developed both size and the ability to be light on its feet.

Endurance Horse

*E*ndurance riding is a sport that is growing fast and the old adage that any 'ordinary horse' can do it is losing ground as standards become higher. It is true that most horses can be made fit enough to cover long distances but that is not what the sport is about. The endurance horse must also be able to keep going at a comparatively high average speed – around 16 kmph (10 mph) for 160 km (100 miles) – and must pass veterinary inspections along the way and at the finish. This calls for a horse of great soundness and courage, with a lean and sinewy physique.

The Arabian is eminently successful but does not provide the complete answer to the problem, as slightly bigger horses with a longer stride and more powerful musculature often prove more successful, especially on faster terrain. In France, where the sport is very popular, purpose-bred horses combining Arabian, Selle Français and Trotter blood are in demand, while in America, where endurance riding was invented, using the old pioneer trails, the Arab/Standardbred cross is popular. Appaloosa, Australian Stock Horse, Andalusian, Welsh Cob, Dales Pony, Trakehner and, of course, the Thoroughbred have all produced successful endurance horses.

DISTINGUISHING FEATURES

At an endurance ride veterinary inspection, the horse's heart rate must quickly recover to not more than 64 beats per minute. It must trot up sound and be passed 'fit to continue' at all stages of the ride, including the finish.

HEIGHT

14-16 h.h.

COLOUR

Any.

CONFORMATION

Lean, with lightweight musculature but a well-proportioned skeletal structure is essential. Strong, dense bone with well-angulated joints, long, muscular thighs and forearms, short cannons, medium-length pasterns and extremely hard, sound feet, well-supported at the heel.

ACTION

Well-balanced, sure-footed, economical and ground-covering.

Falabella

The Falabella is named after the Argentinian family who developed the horse and who, by selling almost no breeding stock, have ensured that it remains a rare and expensive curiosity, which, in view of its very specialized characteristics and the potential for abuse, is certainly no bad thing. The Falabella is a horse in miniature and, unlike the weight-carrying Shetland Pony (even the miniature Shetland), which has strength beyond the capacity of its size, the Falabella is an extremely delicate, fine-boned creature, incapable of carrying any rider, even a small child. Its only use is as a loved family pet.

There appears to be a dominant gene in the Falabella, which, when crossed with bigger breeds, progressively ensures a diminution in size. The true origin of what is best described as a genetic mutation is uncertain, though it is reputed to have come from a small stallion found wandering on his ranch by the grandfather of the current head of the Falabella family, in the last century when tribes of indigenous Indians of Argentina attacked the homes of European settlers.

All colours are permitted, with special accord given to the Appaloosa derivative. The type varies, depending upon the breed used as the original cross with the miniature, and upon inherited conformation details (the latter often show various weaknesses which breeders are gradually trying to eliminate). The Falabella lacks the hardiness of native pony breeds and must be cared for with the same consideration – perhaps more – as the Thoroughbred horse. This means correct feeding and the provision of rugs, stabling and extra heating in winter.

HEIGHT

Maximum 86 cm (34 in).

COLOUR

Any colour is permitted.

CONFORMATION

A horse in miniature, fine-boned, with small feet. It lacks hardiness